UNCONVENTIONAL MEANS

THE DREAM DOWN UNDER

ANNE RICHARDSON WILLIAMS

WITH ABORIGINAL TRADITIONAL STORIES
AS TOLD BY
LORRAINE MAFI-WILLIAMS

PEARLSONG PRESS

NASHVILLE, TN

Unconventional Means: The Dream Down Under
©2000, 2005 Anne Richardson Williams

Pearlsong Press
P.O. Box 58065
Nashville, TN 37205
www.pearlsong.com
1-866-4-A-PEARL

Second edition, revised and updated
from the In Circle Press first edition published in 2000.

ISBN-10: 1-59719-001-2
ISBN-13: 9781597190015

Library of Congress Control Number: 2004097679

Interior artwork by Anne Richardson Williams

Cover design by Peggy Elam. The front cover graphic blending a
middle Tennessee hill and meadow with an image of Uluru (Ayers
Rock, Australia) was created by Anne Richardson Williams.

DEDICATED TO
PEACE, FORGIVENESS,
AND THE
WISDOM ENTRUSTED TO US ALL.

This book is also dedicated to all those who contributed to the making or the telling of these stories: Louis and Jean Williams, Jean Williams Lallement, Chris Williams, Betty Williams Bailey, Lorraine Mafi-Williams and her family, Alex Kidwell, Nancy McMorrow, Suchi and Tom Benjamin, Gloria Mason, Annie Freeman, Peggy Elam, Jennifer Welch, Stephanie Potts, Edine Frohman, and Henry Ambrose.

CONTENTS

GETTING THERE

THERE

ILLUSTRATIONS

IN THE BEGINNING

APRIL 1, 1963

I AM SIXTEEN TODAY. IT'S BEEN FUN. EVERYBODY HAS MADE A BIG deal about it.

Mama gave me a charm for my charm bracelet that says "Sweet Sixteen," and Daddy took me to get my driver's license. He looked really handsome standing there in front of the Highway Patrol Building in a silvery colored suit, waiting while I took the driving part of the test.

I am so happy! Now I can drive!

JUNE 24, 1963

MY FATHER IS DEAD; HE KILLED HIMSELF. THE REST OF us aren't doing so good either.

Nobody wants to talk about it. Can't somebody just tell me why this is happening?

This was supposed to be the best summer of my life. I was going to spend it driving, taking my friends to the club to swim or just cruising up and down the boulevard. Instead I stay in my room most of the time and read and feel like a jerk for thinking about what I am missing out on at a time like this. I bet I will break the record for reading the most books on the summer reading list.

Would my father still be alive if I had done something different? What do we do now, my mother and brother and sister and me? Will we be OK?

JULY 6, 1963

LAST WEEK I READ A BOOK FROM THE SUMMER READING LIST called *On the Beach*, by Nevil Shute, and now I wish that I hadn't. It made me feel worse that I did already.

In the book, atomic fallout has killed everybody in the world except a few people in Australia who are just waiting for their turn. Nobody seems to have any idea how such a thing could be happening. At the end, everybody dies, even the little babies, everybody.

When I think about it, I feel everything get smaller and smaller and then just disappear.

At night, I dream that a giant heart, Daddy's heart, is on the pillow next to my head, pumping away. I want to get away from it, but I can't move.

Heart on Fire

SEPTEMBER 15, 1963

S CHOOL HAS STARTED AGAIN. TODAY I WAS SITTING ON SOME steps on campus trying to last-minute memorize a speech for French class. Suddenly everything got very far away, like looking at the world through the wrong end of a telescope.

I couldn't make my old way of seeing come back. All I could think about was "How will I ever get through school like this?"

At night, I do drawing after drawing of Daddy's heart in flames on the pillow next to me. Nobody wants to talk about them, the drawings, I mean, including me.

One is so scary that it scares me that I did it. After a few days I cut the heart out of it, then put it back with a piece of scotch tape, which makes it scarier than ever, a Frankenstein heart.

But now I can lift that little paper heart like a flap and look through the drawing, and I can see that there is something on the other side of this terrible drawing and the terrible dream and the terrible thing that has happened to my family, and I feel a little better.

And some of the drawings are beautiful.

SEPTEMBER 29, 1963

I DON'T KNOW HOW I COULD HAVE READ ANOTHER BOOK BY NEVIL Shute. I did, though, and I am really glad. It is called *A Town Like Alice* after Alice Springs, Australia.

The story is about an English woman living in Malaysia when World War II breaks out and she is taken prisoner by the Japanese, with other English women and children. Her name is Jean — that is my mother's name, and my sister's. Instead of being put in a prisoner of war camp, the group is forced to march from village to village, every day, for a year or so. A lot of the women and children die, including a friend, whose baby Jean takes care of.

Along the way she meets another prisoner, an Australian man from Alice Springs named Joe. She likes him a lot. She doesn't tell him that the baby isn't hers, so he thinks she is married. He likes her, too, and he steals chickens from a commandant for her and her friends. He gets caught and the Japanese CRUCIFY him, while the women and children are made to watch before they are marched away.

Things get better after that. One of the women believes their good luck is because of Joe and his sacrifice, like Christ's. The women and children who are still alive spend the rest of the war peacefully in a little village near the sea.

When the war ends, Jean goes home to England. Life doesn't interest her very much. Her family is dead and she believes that the Australian died for her. Then one day she inherits money from an uncle whom she barely remembers. She returns to Malaysia with some of her legacy and has a well dug for the villagers who were nice to her during the war.

The three welldiggers tell her that the Australian did not die. She finds him again, and they get married and go to live somewhere in the Outback in Australia. There's not much there when she first arrives. Jean uses her legacy to help create a town where she and her neighbors would want to live. She has in mind a town like Alice, so that is how the book got its name.

There was something on the other side of the terrible things for her, too.

Someday I want to go to Australia and to Alice Springs.

Through the Heart

FURTHER ALONG

JANUARY 1, 1989

A FEW DAYS AGO I FOUND MY OLD JOURNAL, LAST ENTRY dated 1963.Since then I have been scribbling around the idea of bringing my own story up to date.

Picking up the thread of a journal long since dormant might be a bizarre experience, but I feel compelled to try. Surely I can find something to write about, with twenty-six more years of life on Planet Earth as fodder for contemplation.

I regret to inform my much younger self that I haven't made it to Australia. Not yet. I did manage to graduate from George Peabody College in Nashville in 1969 with a B.A in Fine Arts and immediately moved to England, where I lived for four years. As I got on the plane from New York to London I wondered if I was headed in the wrong direction, and consoled myself with the literary fact that the heroine of *A Town Like Alice* was English.

The years in England turned out to be good years, too. There was a big enough mingle of adventure and travel to rosy the ploddingness of my daily life. There was an English boyfriend, Crispin, who came complete with an educated, worldly family that welcomed me into their enclave and contributed civility (as Crispin's mother viewed it) to my unpolished American ways. Crispin's mother taught me how to cook in several languages, and Crispin's father, he of the beautiful voice and loving heart, taught me the value of reading all kinds of literature.

And yet, and yet—even though I was now undeniably more literate, civilized, and could cook, and while I always worked at jobs in England (from waiting tables to working in a print gallery), I had no goals and nothing that smacked of career orientation.

After a rare visit to Tennessee in the middle of a July, it was easy for me to drift back to live in the U.S., noting poetically to myself that I longed again for the liquidness of Southern summer nights. The weather probably did have something to do with my decision to leave England. I love the way the wind blows the leaves to silver before rain will sweep these middle Tennessee hills.

Truthfully, though (imbued as I am with the wisdom of hind-sight—Ha!), I went home riding the hope that returning to my roots would connect me to the rhythm of my own life. Finding that rhythm has turned out to be a much longer and more roundabout (though interesting and often mysterious) journey than I would have wanted to contemplate back then, in the middle 1970s.

After a stopover in New Orleans that lasted a year or so while I worked at Sophie Newcomb College and ate oysters, I was back in Nashville poised for whatever was to come next.

Ta-Da! In the order of appearance what came was: a man named Bill, an artist and builder/designer of great skill; falling in love; a job as a picture framer while I dinked around sporadically with my own artistic urges; a marriage; the cutest little baby boy you ever saw, Alexander, born in 1979; starting my own conservation picture framing business/art gallery, which I would never have imagined myself doing and somehow ended up creating for myself anyway; a divorce and single motherhood, which I had never imagined creating for myself, either.

No need for more specific details of any of the above, as they are all pretty much standard issue for The Human Drama.

I *would* like to point out that interwoven with this parade of events, I became at least semi-conscious of the fact that I am a spiritual being, began to meditate, grappled with the realities of Oneness and Presence and Unconditional Love, and embraced a spiritual community that changes and grows in a delightful dance with my own changing and growing understanding of the life of the spirit.

So, much younger self, are these life experiences ones that you might have chosen for yourself all those years ago, or are you politely suppressing the desire to shriek "EEK, WHAT HAPPENED?"

If the latter, take comfort. I am here to assure you that everything is all right. These years have delivered unto you a mother lode of experiences to understand and grow through and the wisdom to be grateful for (almost) all who were willing to participate in your parade. OK, you did your share of struggling, coping and surviving. You also had some fun and you learned. A lot.

From a girl limited to a white, upward-of-middle-class, Protestant American Southern perspective and to squinting through the wrong end of a telescope, you have become a woman set on being as wide-angled as she can handle. As my friend James would say in celebration, you're the happenin'.

The baby Alex has grown into a humorous and intelligent boy, and through our mutual love of him, his dad and I have healed many of the wounds of divorce.

The business is doing fine. I lament not yet pursuing my own creativity with much fervor, although I like spending my days on intimate terms with other people's art. I know my time will come.

I know for the oddest reason, because I felt a rhythm (the one I came home for?) kickstart one night as I sat in a smallish audience in a smallish room of the Tennessee State Museum, listening to a panel of men and women discuss a collection of early, handmade American maps that laid out the New World in terms of its existing Native American inhabitants. Several of the panelists presented short lectures on the history of maps and the U.S. A cartographer lectured on cartography. A Native American woman talked about Native American rights.

Then an Indian educator named Cornell Pewewardy stood up, commented that Native American children do not learn in a linear way, and began to tap his pencil on the podium and to chant to the beat. To the TAP-tap-tap of the pencil and the sound of Mr. P's voice, I (along with others in the audience, presumably) attempted the somewhat dizzy-making shift to a different mode of engaging.

That is when I felt "it" begin—a rhythm, a beat, like a kind of inner wave rising and falling.

Maybe I thought it would go away when Mr. Pewewardy put his pencil down and went back to his seat. It didn't.

Maybe I thought this rhythm, whatever it is, would only crank up if someone were tapping a pencil and chanting to me. That hasn't proven to be true either. Even on days heavy with a lack of self-motivation, I read a poem or two by Pablo Neruda or Mary Oliver and *voila*—I am inspired to start whisking together the stuff my own dreams are made of.

I AM LAUGHING, MUCH YOUNGER SELF, AT THE IDEA THAT YOU are now rolling your eyes and thinking you grew up to be a total nut case. That's the good news!

Life is magical and—oh, no, I can't resist the opportunity to say this—the beat goes on!

AUGUST 15, 1989

Although Australia is always at the top of my list of places to go, I can't seem to plan the trip. Australia will have to happen to me.

Now, all these years later, I have seen something that puts the heart back into going there, especially to Alice Springs. What I saw was a calendar picture of Ayers Rock sitting majestically in the middle of the Australian desert.

Ayers Rock is red, a deeper red than the orange red of the desert around it, underneath a thin violet skin that glows. Humped up through hundreds, maybe thousands, of square miles of sand like a whale at sea, the "Rock" is part of something much bigger, something hidden. It is the heart of Australia.

The information blurb on the calendar says Ayers Rock also has another name — Uluru — and that it is sacred to Aboriginal people.

The closest town of any size, across two hundred miles of desert, is Alice Springs.

JANUARY 15, 1993

I JUST FINISHED READING STEVEN MCFADDEN'S *ANCIENT VOICES, Current Affairs: The Legend of the Rainbow Warriors.* In chapter eight I saw a photograph of Lorraine Mafi-Williams, an Aboriginal elder, and thought to myself, "Look, it's my sister. We even have the last name."

I showed her picture to my son, Alex, and said, "Don't you think we look alike?" and he said, "Mom, you're crazy."

It *is* crazy, I think so, too, that when I look at her, I see myself.

She is also called Alinta, Woman of Fire. In the back of the book there is a list of addresses for the other elders mentioned, although there is none for her.

She talks about Uluru, Ayers Rock. In her tribal lands there is a sacred mountain called Wollumbin, the first place in Australia that the sun touches each morning. The story goes that deep within the mountain is a giant rose quartz crystal. It is awakened every day by the warmth of the sun's rays and sends energy to Uluru, which passes it on to Tibet. This is an ancient connection. Tibetan lamas have been coming to Uluru for prayer and ceremony since the early 1980s.

She talks about how her people originally came from a planet that blew up, as she says, when its time came.

In meditation a few years ago, I saw a planet exploding in a fiery ball and said, "Oh my God! Is this my fault?" I cried for days, overwhelmed by the feeling that I had made a terrible mistake. I can't explain it. Meanwhile, my everyday life went on exactly as before.

The summer that I read Nevil Shute's books, the summer my father died and I first decided to go to Australia, that summer my world blew up, too. What I saw that day in meditation, what I felt, was deeper even than that.

I can only guess there was something I needed to know.

LORRAINE MAFI-WILLIAMS,
ALSO KNOWN AS
ALINTA, WOMAN OF FIRE.
Photo by Matthew Tung originally published in
Ancient Voices, Current Affairs: The Legend of the Rainbow Warriors
by Steven McFadden.
Reprinted with permission.

January 16, 1993

People and places in Australia often have two names, a "white" name and an aboriginal name, a legal name and an elemental name—Ayers Rock or Uluru, Mount Warning or Wollumbin, Lorraine Mafi-Williams or Alinta.

Underneath the veneer of civilization, I hear an ancient Australia breathing, alive and well.

OCTOBER 25, 1993

I CLOSED ON THE SALE OF MY BUSINESS TODAY.

I loved doing what I did for a long time, for years, until all the challenges began to feel like the same old challenges and I was crawling home at the end of every work day with my battery drained dry. Thank you, THANK YOU, to the someone who finally showed up to buy me out.

Now I sit here with my face flushed beet-red—five parts celebration and seven parts the mild panic that comes from letting go and not knowing what happens next.

Just last week, I stood weeping in a parking lot with a friend, asking out loud for some more knowledgeable aspect of myself—which I am willing to actually exist—to let me in on why I was really going through with all this. After a few long minutes punctuated by my sniffles and soothing noises from the friend, a pleasant calmness settled around me like a cozy blanket and I knew (again) that I was doing the right thing.

Not so much the big WHY of it, just that it was the right thing.

November 2, 1995

A FRIEND INVITED A GROUP OF US TO MEET A FORTUNE teller, a man who reads lightning-struck cedar sticks to tell the future. His gift comes from a Native American grandmother.

The sticks say that right before my fiftieth birthday I will cross a lot of water, a sea, perhaps, to meet a woman, and when I return, everything in my life will change.

FEBRUARY 15, 1996

TODAY, IN MEDITATION, I WAS HOLDING A LARGE CRYSTAL, A five-sided crystal, and asked to be connected to the heart of the Earth. With my inner sight I saw the energy of the crystal streak downwards, bounce like a satellite beam off something at the center of the earth and POW—I "ran" into Lorraine Mafi-Williams, the Aboriginal elder I had read about.

The force of the connection startled me, knocked the breath out of me. I had no idea that meditation and inner connections could be so—physical.

I could see Lorraine clear as day, and she wasn't alone. There was another, a being of light, just to her right.

I have no idea what this means.

JULY 6, 1996

THE FIRST TIME I FELT MYSELF BEING ENERGETICALLY connected to Lorraine Mafi-Williams, I wasn't expecting it. Now when I try to connect intentionally, nothing much happens.

I have no idea what this means.

DECEMBER 15, 1996

I T APPEARS THAT THE TRIP FORETOLD BY THE LIGHTNING-STRUCK cedar sticks isn't going to happen.

I have scheduled myself to co-teach a Book Arts class as part of a curriculum based on the ancient Mystery Schools. The class will go from February all the way through to May, a month or so past my fiftieth birthday. Brochures have been printed and mailed, materials for the class have been bought.

I will be doing work that I want to do, with people I want to work with. However…??

Am I off track?

January 4, 1997

A T FIRST I COULDN'T BELIEVE IT. NOBODY SIGNED UP FOR the class.

I have been wandering around the house for three or four days, a wad of disappointment, wondering what convinced me that teaching the class was what I was supposed to do. At the same time I have also been feeling something elusive, something fugitive until today, when I finally said right out loud, "Oh. Well, I might as well go to Australia."

I have an inheritance from my Aunt Betty to help pay for the trip. How coincidental is that? It's a plot twist straight out of Neville Shute that a legacy from a relative makes this journey possible for me.

I have about three weeks to get organized.

So this is how I will get to Australia, by entering the experience through the back door, more or less. It's an "A" trip — Anne goes to Australia, to Alice Springs and to Ayers Rock. To Adelaide, too, because the only two people I know in Australia are Karen and Peter Wilson, whom I met when they lived in Nashville for a few years while Peter was doing research at Vanderbilt.

And there is something else, although I can hardly think about it, it seems so unlikely—I would like to meet Lorraine Mafi-Williams, Alinta, Woman of Fire, in person.

JANUARY 5, 1997

THE HEROINE'S JOURNEY IN *A Town Like Alice* LED HER TO use her legacy to create a completely different way of life for herself and her new community.

When I peer down my version of the well to ask the three welldiggers a question, I hope the answer I receive will grow choices as brave and rewarding as hers.

Getting There

January 8, 1997

I BOUGHT AN AIRLINE TICKET TODAY, FROM AN AGENT WHOSE office is on the fourth floor of an eight-sided building, one of the tallest buildings on Nashville's Music Row. While the agent worked on the way to get me to Australia and back again, I stared out the window next to her desk, at first at the emptiness of a big blue winter sky and then at a red-tailed hawk. Round and round the hawk went, over rooftops and treetops, gliding and dipping on its huge wings for an hour or more, until finally I was booked to fly, on the fifth of February, landing first in Adelaide. The hawk swooped by one last time and disappeared.

As I was leaving, I asked the agent if the red-tailed hawk was a familiar sight in that area, and she said, "What hawk?"

"The one that was flying right outside the window for so long," I answered, and she said, "Oh, I didn't see it."

As the red-tailed hawk is my birth totem in some Native

American traditions, I am taking it as a sign of good luck that one was with me as I begin this trip.

JANUARY 15, 1997

NOW I HAVE A GIANT MAP OF AUSTRALIA AND A STACK OF travel guides, and every day for the last week or so has been dedicated to flipping back and forth, relentlessly, through first one guide book, then another. Back and forth, back and forth, from Dubbo, Brisbane and Kuranda to Hobart, Cape Wilson and Flinders Island.

I also have (found curiously placed in the bookstore travel section) a reference book called *Aboriginal Mythology* by a man named Mudrooroo. I read it every day. I like to follow the connections that appear at the bottom of each entry — from the Arrernte people and Uluru, *see* the Dreamtime; from the Adnyamathanha people and the Flinders Ranges, *see* Akurra Serpent and rainmaking; from Goanna Headland, *see* floods, the Bundjalung National Park, the Rainbow Serpent and Creation Myths.

It surprised me to find an entry for Lorraine Mafi-Williams. Is she a myth?

The book says that she lives in Byron Bay on the New South Wales coast, or at least she did in 1994, when the book was published. Byron Bay is in her clan lands, in Bundjalung country.

JANUARY 18, 1997

A T NIGHT I STUDY THE MAP OF AUSTRALIA ON MY WALL. The flat, fleshy brown of the central desert has begun to look like a breast whose nipple is the McDonnell Ranges. In the south, a group of fish-shaped lakes leap playfully from the Great Australian Bight into the Outback, above Port Augusta. The eastern coastline is mountainous green and hairy with place names.

January 20, 1997

THERE IS TILL NOT A DEFINITE ROUTE FOR MY JOURNEY, AND the guidebooks aren't helping much. They do their job, making each place they mention sound like the place to go.

I feel as if I am waiting for some deeper rhythm to begin, although I have no sense of it yet, and February 5 is getting closer. In the meantime, every well-meaning suggestion from friends and family about where to go and what to see, and particularly the comment "You're going by *yourself?!*" drives my anxiety about this trip up another notch or two.

And I smoke— after, oh my God, twenty years! I feel less anxious when I do, although I am told that smoking doesn't ground me, that it just makes me smaller. Have I lost my mind?

Suddenly I remember something from my childhood when I was at camp, the night I was sleepwalking and woke myself up at the door to my cabin, screaming, "Help me! Somebody help me. I'm lost!"

I woke up everybody else in camp, too. I was too embarrassed to go to breakfast the next morning, and stayed in bed with a pillow over my head for the rest of the day.

JANUARY 21, 1997

AS MY ANXIETY FLUCTUATES FROM A MILD CASE OF butterflies to a flat-out, high-grade existential angst, I remind myself that while Lorraine Mafi-Williams may be hard, may be impossible, to find, Ayers Rock won't be; and I can always go to the beach. In the meantime, I am not completely without resources. I can sit and breathe. I can count on meditation.

Meditation is the best decision-making tool I have. Sitting on the cushion in front of my little altar, I have received practical solutions for just about everything, even raising children and selling a business.

So today I tackled the issue of gifts, because let's say I go to Australia and actually meet Lorraine Mafi-Williams. I would want to have something to offer her in the traditional way as a thank you for the teachings. And, please, something lightweight, so I won't get tired of carrying it around.

I didn't have to wait long for an answer. Just as I closed my eyes, I saw the frog on the front of a T-shirt from Radnor Lake.[1] Excellent! A T-shirt weighs practically nothing, it won't take up much room in a suitcase, and Radnor Lake is a natural area in Nashville that is loved by a lot of people.

"Anything else?" I asked. Immediately I saw another T-shirt. This time it was black with a Harley-Davidson eagle on it.

"I can't give a Harley-Davidson T-shirt as a sacred offering to an Aboriginal elder," I muttered to myself.

On the other hand, the process is the process, even if it doesn't match my sense of how things ought to be. I will be getting one of those shirts, too.

JANUARY 24, 1997

AN EMAIL FROM STEVEN MCFADDEN HAS ARRIVED. HE HAS sent a telephone number for Lorraine, remarking that it was three or four years old and he didn't know if it was still good. He wished me good luck.

I decided to call the authors of *The Circle is Sacred*, another book that features Lorraine, to ask if they knew a phone number or an address where I might reach her. The woman's voice on the other end of the line paused, then said, "She is an Aboriginal woman." From her response, I infer that I am being naive about something.

The voice did give me an email address for someone in Sydney who might be of help, and I have sent a message. There has been no reply.

I haven't been able to reach Karen and Peter Wilson by phone to let them know I am on my way. After all these years of telling them I was coming, wouldn't it be ironic if I make it to Adelaide and never see them?

Anyway, no matter how it works out, even the possibility of seeing them is helping to get me there.

JANUARY 26, 1997

NYTHING THAT MIGHT HELP ME FIND THE WAY AROUND
Australia is interesting to me, so at the recommendation of
Suzee Benjamin, my longtime teacher and friend, I went
to see Chris Faulconer[2] for a session of shamanic journeying,

In a quiet little room I lay peacefully, eyes closed, on a massage
table while Chris suggested images to get me started and bring my
focus inward. She asked questions every once in a while to move
things along.

Where was I? I was walking under a bright, blue-white sky along
the curve of a crescent-shaped beach. I could look down and see my
bare feet and feel the hard-packed sand. I could hear the waves and
the scalloped fizz of the incoming tide.

Was there anyone with me? Yes, Lorraine and another woman,
who was tiny and dark-skinned. The tiny woman showed me a
stone that was glowing in her cupped palm as brightly as a live coal.

She told me to feed the dolphins. In my hand appeared a can of small silver fish and I threw them, one by one, to dolphins leaping in the waves just offshore.

The tiny woman, I know who she is. She's a Bundjalung elder mentioned in *Ancient Voices, Current Affairs.* Her name is Mary Wilson, and she was her clan's last custodian for the dolphins.

Now I feel like I am getting somewhere, that important connections are being made.

I had a session with Suzee,[3] too, where, once again while stretched out comfortably on a massage table in Nashville, I took a walk along a beach, this one stretching for miles under a bright, bright sun. Lorraine and Mary were there, too.

And, silhouetted against the distant rocky headland, another figure approached, a figure full of light and dressed, Christ-like, in sandals and a long robe. A messenger whose presence was the message, telling me that if I pay attention, everything will come together in the way that it's meant.

JANUARY 28, 1997

ACCORDING TO THE GUIDEBOOKS, THERE ARE A LOT OF
places in Australia that have a particular association with
dolphins.

I don't feel compelled to go to any of them, although I feel as
if I should.

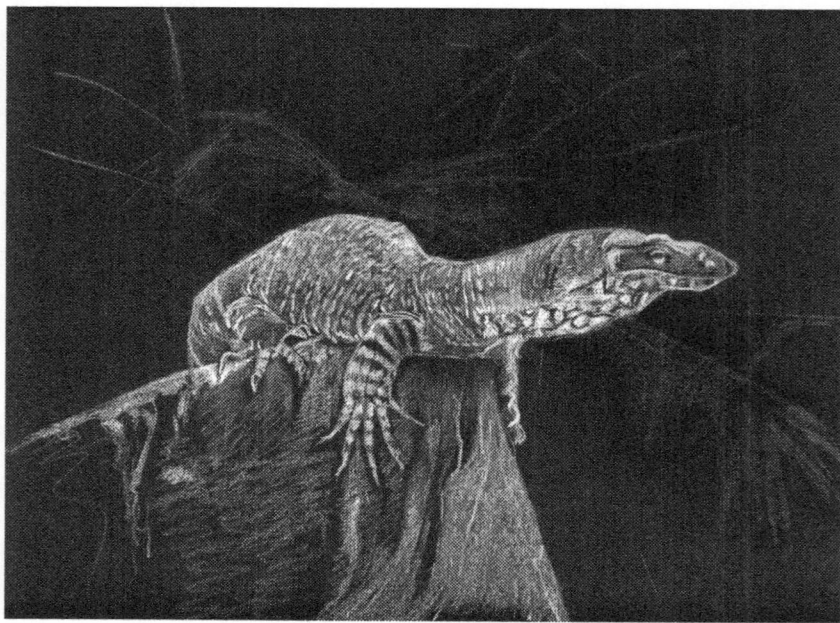

Goanna

January 30, 1997

L ast night I dreamed that I changed my name to Goanna.

The *Aboriginal Mythology* book tells me this morning that Goanna is an Australian lizard with connections to the Dreamtime and to the legends of the Rainbow Serpent.

I put my hand on the big map on the wall and could feel my journey beginning to form itself, moving up from Adelaide in the south to Uluru, following the Goanna stories across the Australian landscape, then turning eastward to the Goanna Headland, which is in the Bundjalung traditional lands.

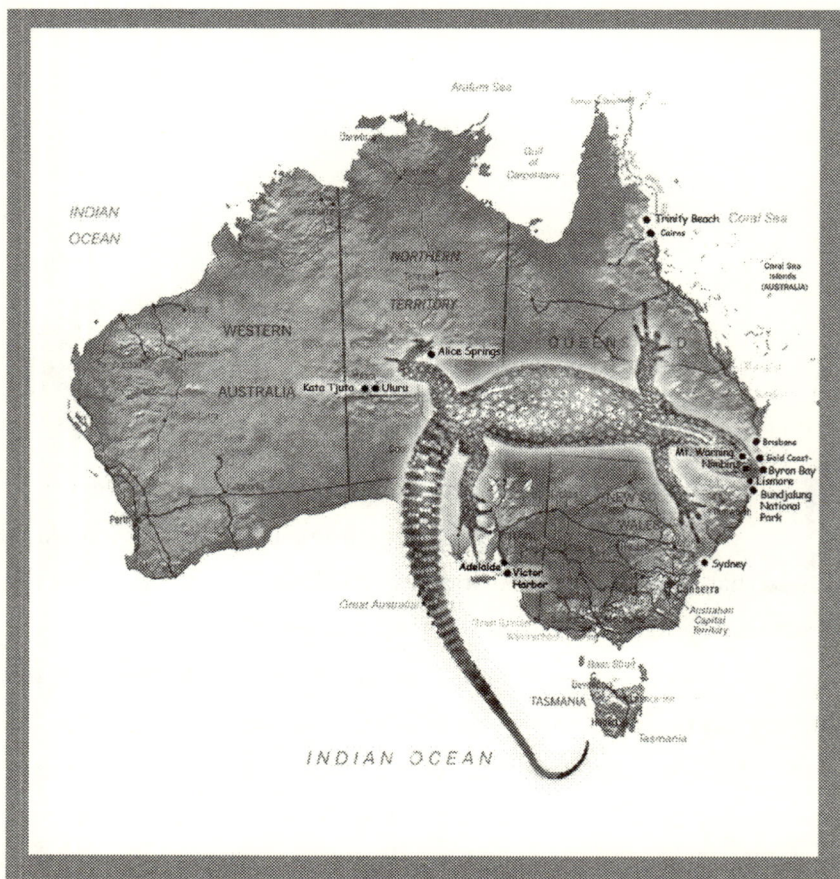

Goanna Map

FEBRUARY 2, 1997

JUST A FEW MORE DAYS AND I AM OFF.

Suzee came by and gave me a little medallion to wear. On one side is the image of Christ and on the other, one of Mary. A little mother energy for the journey, she said.

She also mentioned that on a recent trip to a bookstore, she had been unusually drawn to a book about Sai Baba, a great spiritual leader in India. I don't know much about him.

"Just keep Sai Baba in mind," Suzee suggested. "The author of the book is a man named Howard Murphet and he is from Australia."

FEBRUARY 3, 1997

KAREN WILSON HAS CALLED FROM ADELAIDE. SHE HAD JUST received the express letter I sent and wanted to let me know that they are expecting me.

FEBRUARY 5, 1997

THIS IS IT.
I see a safe journey.
I see a safe return.

THERE

FEBRUARY 7, 1997

AFTER A LAYOVER IN LOS ANGELES THAT WAS SO LONG I took a city bus to Malibu for a walk on the beach, I am at last in Adelaide.

When the plane landed first in Sydney earlier this morning, the sunrise was full of rainbows.

FEBRUARY 8, 1997

I CAN'T IMAGINE A LESS CONVENIENT TIME FOR ME TO ARRIVE IN the Wilsons' household.

Summer vacation has just ended here. There are four Wilson children, all in different schools, and this is their first week back. Karen is juggling the different schedules and events while trying to find time to visit with me. Peter works as hard as ever at a medical practice that includes an island, where he flies once a week to spend two days.

Despite everything, they seem genuinely happy to see me.

One afternoon Karen and I went to the zoo, and on the next, we drove through the Adelaide hills to Mount Lofty. Mount Lofty is the ear of a sleeping giant. The rolling hills above Adelaide are covered with grape vineyards, and every tree we see is eucalyptus. With two hundred fifty varieties, Karen says it is Australia's most common kind of tree. The mossy, fishnet-like appearance of eucalyptus leaves as they blow in the wind reminds me where I am.

The weather is very odd, from South Australia northward. For a month or more, torrential rains have been falling across large sections of the interior, usually one of the driest regions in the world. Flash floods continue to wash out roads and railroad lines, and the news is full of stories of travelers who have been stranded for days in remote areas further inland.

February 9, 1997

A COOL AND RAINY SUNDAY, MY SECOND FULL DAY IN Australia.

This morning we were on our way to Victor Harbor, a resort town on the coast just south of Adelaide. Karen and Henry (one of the Wilson children) were sitting in back with Henry's friend. I was up front and Peter was driving, through the grassy coastal hills for an hour or so before turning onto a narrow road that went steeply downward, between high banks of trees and fencerows, to Victor Harbor and the sea.

About halfway down, when we were headed for the embankment going fifty miles an hour, I noticed that Peter was asleep.

I yelled and he woke up and we didn't hit the bank—on *that* side of the road. Somehow the car flipped over and skidded on its roof across the road to smash into the embankment on the other side.

Crossing the road seemed to take forever, all the time in the world, the five of us dangling upside down like bats in our seatbelts while I listened to a curious, detached voice in my head say things like "Hmmm, upside down in the Land Down Under? Does that make me right side up? I wonder what this means?"

Well, I am wondering what this means, too.

By some miracle human injuries were minor, just a few stitches in Peter's shoulder. The car is trashed.

Our day in Victor Harbor turned out to be a visit to the local hospital, a long look around the car repair shop, and a really expensive taxi ride back to Adelaide.

FEBRUARY 10, 1997

LAST NIGHT I DREAMED THAT I WAS MOVING VERY FAST DOWN A hill on a road like the one to Victor Harbor. No matter how hard I tried to slow down by digging in my heels, I couldn't stop. The road turned into a ski jump and I was launched, flying through the air over the town and heading out to sea.

Much to my amazement, I woke up this morning feeling happy and relieved. Surely the worst thing that can happen already has?

I think Karen and Peter are feeling guilty, afraid they have spoiled the beginning of my trip, so I need to let them know I am all right and that, at least for me, wrecking the car appears to have a silver lining.

I have left behind, on the road to Victor Harbor, any illusions that this will be a normal vacation. Now I am ready to follow my nose across Australia.

FEBRUARY 11, 1997

O<small>N LEAVING</small> A<small>DELAIDE, MY PLAN WAS TO FOLLOW THE</small>
Goanna and Serpent Dreamtime stories a few hundred
kilometers north, to Wilpena Pound in the Flinders
Ranges, traditional home of the Adnyamathanha people. Wilpena
Pound is a natural enclosure, formed by the eroded remnants of
massive mountains, and looks like the jaws and teeth of an ancient
emerging beast. The rim is said to be the bodies of two Akurras, or
Rainbow Serpents, a male and a female.

The elemental forces of Akurra (and also Goanna) are associated
with the making of rain in the Dreamtime, and are shaping my trip
in ways I hadn't counted on. Because of the rain, the Flinders Ranges
are temporarily inaccessible.

I am staying in Adelaide a few extra days, hoping for a change
in weather.

FEBRUARY 12, 1997

I talked by phone to Biannca Pace today. She is the person in Sydney I considered my best bet for finding Lorraine Mafi-Williams.

Biannca has not heard from her in months.. She believes Lorraine might be living in a Sydney suburb. She has no direct way to contact her.

My afternoon was spent in the State Library of South Australia, a big modern building among all the classical architecture in downtown Adelaide. There was an enormous Aboriginal reference book that mentioned Lorraine and said she lived in Byron Bay. Once again, the book was at least three years old.

There was also a listing for several movies Lorraine has made, one based on a traditional tale called *Eelemarni*. *Eelemarni* was not available in Adelaide. The woman at the desk checked the database for all the other state libraries and said I could see it in Sydney.

I am having a lot of fun, following clues, tracking down information. I feel like a mapmaker in uncharted territory, although sometimes I feel like a stalker.

FEBRUARY 13, 1997

ON A WHIM, I JUMPED ON THE TROLLEY THAT HAS BROUGHT me to Adelaide's city beach, called Glenelg, where I have been lying in the sand, fully clothed, for hours. As Glenelg is on the south coast of Australia, wouldn't it be something if I could stand up, turn a little in the right direction, and see beyond the curve of the earth to Antarctica, the next continent over?

It is nice here, a pretty little community of its own, with an area for shops and snug houses that line the streets fingering out from the beach walk. Nearby, in the hard sand just above the tideline, is a drawing of a dolphin with a smooth green beachstone for an eye and the name "Alex" scrawled underneath.

When my son Alex was three years old, we went to Florida on a family vacation and visited SeaWorld. Alex had gotten way too much sun, and we ought to have been in a cool motel room. Instead we were standing with a group around the lip of a dolphin pool when one of the dolphins started swimming round and round close to the sides of the pool, gathering moss into a ball. Suddenly the dolphin stopped and tossed the ball of moss to Alex. Alex threw it back to the dolphin, who tossed it back to Alex and so on, toss, toss, toss, toss.

At home I have a photograph of them, Alex and the dolphin, playing "Toss the Moss." In the picture's foreground, Alex is laughing, his face so blotchy red and swollen that it hurts just to look at it. In the background, the dolphin is laughing, too.

THIS MUST BE THE DAY FOR DOLPHIN STORIES, BECAUSE NOW I AM remembering another family vacation in Florida, when I was a little girl of five or six, maybe seven.

A man and his wife whose last name was Love, friends of my parents, had towed me out into the ocean swells so I could try riding the surf back to the beach on a little rubber raft. Although we weren't very far out, the water was deep enough to be over my head.

The heave of the ocean kept knocking me off the raft, which made Mr. and Mrs. Love laugh, and one or the other of them would reach out and grab me and shove me back on. They were on their honeymoon and fun to be with. I didn't mind as much as usual that my bathing suit was full of sand.

So I there I was, flailing around in the water and trying one more time to clamber aboard the little-red-on-one-side-blue-on-the-other raft, when Mr. Love said abruptly, "We are going in."

He scooped me up onto the raft and started towing it toward the shore. On the other side of me was his wife, and each of them had an arm laid protectively over my back, to keep me in place.

"What's wrong?" I asked, and Mr. Love said, "Nothing. It's just time to go in."

Along the shoreline I could see a lot of people, running and waving their arms over their heads in a wild kind of way, and my father was walking really fast from the direction of our cabin. Suddenly, in the ocean close around us, something churned, something whirled and thrashed.

Mr. and Mrs. Love just kept walking, not panicked, not desperate, but determined, twisting and pushing their way through the water, working hard to stay upright with their feet on the bottom, towing me between them. Because of them, I never once felt afraid—not once, not even after they finally pulled me and the raft right out of the surf and kept going until we were high and dry on the beach surrounded by people, including my parents, with terrified looks on their faces.

Some were crying, and I listened to everyone talking about the pair of sharks that had been circling us, about their big fins cutting the water so close to us, getting ready to attack, and about the school of dolphins that arrived like a miracle in the nick of time to form a ring of safety around the three of us and force the sharks back out to sea.

It was a miracle, and I never felt afraid until I looked around and saw my father with a gun in his hand. That scared me.

A DRAWING OF A DOLPHIN IN THE SAND HAS ME FLOODED WITH memories.

I wonder why today?

FEBRUARY 14, 1997

THE STORMS AND FLOODS CONTINUE.

The road to Wilpena Pound is still washed out, so I have booked a ticket on the Ghan, a train that will take me directly from Adelaide north through the desert to Alice Springs in the Red Center, as they call it here. I still think of it as a nipple.

FEBRUARY 15, 1997

THE MOST COLORFUL PART OF THE GHAN HAS TURNED OUT to be its past.

Named after Afghani camel trains that pioneered transport in the Outback, the original Ghan had a catalogue of drawbacks, like a set of tracks that had been laid (in dry weather) through hundreds of miles of flood plain and consequently tended to wash out while the train was en route. A trip from Adelaide to Alice Springs might thus have lasted anywhere from fifty hours to ten days, depending on the weather.

The efficient and uneventful New Ghan, in which I am traveling, will complete the same journey in about twenty hours. It follows a different route and snakes across the desert on higher ground, through mile after mile of red sand and scrub trees.

The sun has already set in a line of beautiful rainbow color along the pancake-flat horizon. Now the train windows frame an absolute night, with rarely a twinkling light from human settlement to interrupt it.

To pass the time, I drink tea in the lounge car and say "Where are you going?" "Where have you been?" and "How long are you here for?" over and over again to German and Canadian couples and a Japanese teenager.

I slept for a while on a bunk that felt like a row of airplane seats and had a dream that I was looking at my left foot and trying to decide which of my two smaller toes to cut off. In the dream, it was important to be sure and leave the one that would keep me most in balance.

As I wait for the sun to rise again, I am reading Robert Lawlor's *Voices of the First Day: Awakening in the Aboriginal Dreamtime,* a book I bought in the museum in Cherokee, North Carolina. It has information about songlines.

In the Aboriginal Dreamtime, says Lawlor, totemic Ancestors traveled across the unformed surface of the Earth, singing the world into existence, shaping the land by their actions as they moved, sleeping and dreaming the adventures of the next day. Having completed their tasks, the ancestors deposited their vibratory essences in the Earth at sites along their paths before releasing themselves into the Earth and into the sky. The full spectrum of these energies, existing as various colors, frequencies or powers, is often referred to symbolically as the Rainbow Serpent.

The mythic events of the Dreamtime stories, Lawlor continues, occur along paths that stretch in all directions, crisscrossing the entire continent of Australia. The Aboriginal songlines are the maps, recorded in song, for these dreaming tracks. No one group "owns" (knows the songs for) a complete songline, but only a portion, thereby creating a network of communication among clans normally separated by great distances. These songlines correspond to ley lines, a concept that describes the subtle flow of current in the Earth's electromagnetic field.

The songlines also correlate with the grid system that Lorraine Mafi-Williams refers to in her interview with Steven McFadden in *Ancient Voices, Current Affairs*. She declares that the purpose for the Aboriginal people coming to the Earth from the stars was to maintain the health of this system.

FEBRUARY 16, 1997

I AM IN ALICE SPRINGS.

At 10:30 a.m. on this hot summer morning, the Ghan rolled through a gap in the long crescent shape of the McDonnell Ranges and along the track to a small industrial-looking train station. Because of the weather, our arrival was the first in several weeks, and mushroom-y clouds with dark underbellies were already growing again along the northern horizon.

I milled around in a blistering heat with the other passengers, looking for luggage, waiting my turn for a taxi, and giving the driver the name of a motel I had found in a *Lonely Planet* guide. We set off through a maze of prefab-looking buildings and turned left on Todd Street, where a large crowd of black people lapped over the sidewalk in front of an Aboriginal Services building. The taxi driver bullied a way through, honking the car horn.

"If I were you, I'd find me another motel," he said angrily, snarling his comments at me over his shoulder. "Not safe down here with all these goddammed Abos."

I don't remember what he said after that. I had gone blank, then flushed and red, suspicious of what I had missed while reading Nevil Shute all those years ago.

"This motel will be fine," I answered finally. It turned out to be a little shabby, but I was happier to put some distance between me and the cabdriver's point of view than to look for another place to stay.

After settling into a room, I walked back through the crowds along Todd Street — a little nervously (how did Aboriginal people feel about white people in Alice Springs?) — to a public telephone in the center of town, so I could call Alex back home in Tennessee and say, "Hi, I'm here."

The line was so clear, he could have been on the next street over.

FEBRUARY 17, 1997

EVERYONE IN TOWN IS HAVING A PROBLEM WITH THE RAIN. Everyone is having a problem with the flies, which an Aboriginal man at the Cultural Center informed me had arrived with the white man, or, to be more exact, with the dung piles of the white man's cattle.

The heat is relentless. Large groups of black-skinned people sit in the crisp circles of shade under all the trees in the little city park. Although I long to get out of the sun (currently shining in a cloudless sky), I don't have the courage to find out if I would be welcomed among them.

The air-conditioned bars downtown are so jammed that the drinkers — mostly white-skinned, beer in hand — spill out onto the sidewalks. Along the banks of the flooded Todd River, the breezy groves of Red Gums are Aboriginal sacred areas and off-limits to everyone else. So I retreat mid-day to the motel pool. It seems a bizarre luxury surrounded by so much remote and uninhabited desert. Even more bizarre to me is that I am usually the only one in it.

WHAT A CURIOUS PLACE ALICE SPRINGS HAS TURNED OUT TO BE.

Just to the north are a (the) natural spring and the junction of two rivers, now known as the Charles and the Todd. To the south and east is a graceful curve of desert hills, an arm of the McDonnell Ranges. For the sizable Aboriginal community that remains here, this is Mparntwe, since ancient times a sacred gathering place, which was left just as it was created by the Ancestral Beings until the 1880s, when white men arrived bringing the telegraph lines.

Those early pioneers were the first wave of a civilization that had been separated by thousands of years from its hunter-gatherer roots, and for just as long from a belief in the divinity of Mother Earth. They were also motivated by economics. As had happened elsewhere, they saw sacred land as empty land, and claimed it for the Crown. So here at Mparntwe there is also "The Alice," a modern and utilitarian little town with a thriving bar scene, shops selling T-shirts and didgeridoos, and a handful of tourist attractions.

As I see it, Mparntwe and Alice Springs are not connected. They do not blend, meld, or weave together; rather, they somehow exist separately in the same place, making a walk around town a very weird experience. Mounded desert sites associated with the Dreamtime butt up against grocery store parking lots, and the groups of Aboriginals under the shade trees seem to belong to the ancient time, before there was a city park or the center of a town. The sacred groves of Red River Gums, which manage to look peaceful and sun-dappled, are completely hemmed in by a pair of roads and a constant stream of traffic.

Last night, I dreamed about the Red River Gums. In the dream, a black hand took mine and led me down to the riverbank, where, nearby, two teenaged boys were swimming and a middle-aged man was standing waist deep, washing his clothes. The river churned. The water was red with desert sand. On the shady white trunks of the Gum trees, I could read signs that said, "Aboriginal Sacred Site. Access Denied."

Adding to the oddity of Alice Springs and Mparntwe is the presence of Pine Gap, a top-secret American military base that is located just on the outskirts of town. Nobody knows exactly what happens there. There are plenty of rumors.

Pine Gap is something else I didn't read about in Nevil Shute.

FEBRUARY 18, 1997

THE CLOUDBURSTS FURTHER NORTH CONTINUE TO FLOOD the rivers and limit travel. The crowds in the bars and restaurants are anxious to get to Uluru, or on the road out of town. I spend the time swimming round and round the concrete island in the center of the motel pool, like the dolphins and sharks in the tanks at SeaWorld.

The pool has turned out to be a good place to contemplate Robert Lawlor's understanding that "...the Aboriginal people have no concept of the Fall, no sense of being separated from the Divine. In the traditional way, the Dreamtime legends are sung and danced every day, the ritual dances and songs representing the movement, from dream to action, that created the world. Through these activities, the elemental forces and creative energies of the planet are daily renewed and the people are in touch with and honor their sacred purpose here on earth."

Lawlor writes that our cycle of civilization gives every indication that it is completing itself. Perhaps we still have an opportunity to fold into the understanding of who we are one of the deepest collective memories of our race, the Aborigine's rituals, beliefs and cosmology.

FEBRUARY 20, 1997

THERE WERE HEAVY STORMS IN THE DESERT ON SUNDAY NIGHT. On Monday morning, floodwaters came howling along the Finke riverbed and swamped the bridge across the one road from Alice Springs to Uluru. The tour buses, including mine, were making U-turns at the riverbank and cruising the flat one hundred miles back to Alice Springs. Because of all the rain, the desert looks opulent and juicy green with new growth.

The flooding cancelled the three-day hiking and camping expedition I had booked. This morning I left Alice Springs again with a different group, in the desert-worthy, military-looking vehicle of another touring company. There are fourteen of us, people of all ages, twenty-one to sixty-something, and different nationalities: Italian, Swiss, German, Japanese, Korean, Canadian, American, Dutch and Australian. The wild Finke River was back in its banks, so we bumped across the debris-strewn bridge without mishap.

On the other side of the river, the road ran straight as a plumb line. After a while, a cluster of curiously rounded shapes appeared at the horizon, revealing themselves mile by mile as the Olgas, our first destination. The Aboriginal name is Kata Tjuta, Place of Many Heads, a sacred site. The Kata Tjuta is said to be a female place, about whose sacred rituals little is known. Only a small part is open to tourists, the Valley of the Wind, where we spent the morning wandering through one mysterious, narrow, red-rock canyon after another.

All around us, cloud shadows floated silently across the weathered stone skin of the Heads, while the Kata-Tjuta held its stories secret in a vibrant stillness. Our path rose continually upward toward an exuberant sky and a knife-edged pass, where we found a springfed pool surrounded by wildflowers, small trees and the twitter of birds —sounds and sights that seemed out of timing with the rocks and searing heat. From there a scrabbly path descended precipitously to the desert floor. By mid-afternoon, we were back on the bus and on the way to Uluru.

LATER

THE AIR-CONDITIONING IN THE VAN HAS STOPPED WORKING. WE ARE all droopy and limp from the heat and blasted by the wind from the open windows.

To pass the time, I tell stories about Uluru and Mount Wollumbin to the college-aged Canadian woman sitting next to me. Her name is Karina. I tell her that, according to Robert Lawlor, songlines are universal and we follow them, even unconsciously, as we make our

The Kata Tjuta

way through life. I tell her that, according to Bruce Chatwin's book *The Songlines*, if you are following your songline, everyone you meet is your brother, because your songline is their songline, too.

I also tell her that there is a belief that all the songlines that crisscross Australia, perhaps the world, come together at Uluru; and that my trip is the shape of a Goanna that formed itself across a map of Australia after I had a dream.

In the middle distance ahead of us, the shape of Uluru changes and shifts as we move toward it. Somewhere I have read (Lawlor?) that Aboriginal people have no concept of "over there." Everything is "here," expanding from the center. As there is no sense of separation from the Divine, there is no sense of separation from the self. In the vastness of the desert, I attempt expanding my "here" to include Uluru.

At Uluru

Uluru is both the visible nub of a sedimentary layer of sandstone and feldspar, formed by eons of erosion and the tilting of the Earth's surface, and the unique creation of the Dreamtime Ancestors. Its presence is such that we might have been one mile away from Uluru or twenty, there was no way to tell, when our van lurched to a stop in the middle of desert scrub and spinifex. We were just in time for the spectacle of sunset at the "Rock."

Already alight with the sun's last rays, scarred and magnificent, Uluru hummed and flared from orange to red to violet, then turned quietly gray, cool against the evening sky. A little sigh of wind tousled the scrub bushes, and suddenly the desert, so still and elusive just a moment before, erupted with activity, with people walking, with the sound of engines being started, and lines of buses and cars moving off in every direction.

Overarched by an enormous Outback canopy of newly visible stars, our van nosed its way through the post-spectacle traffic, passing monstrous tour buses and a group of Japanese men and women who were eating by candlelight from linen-covered tables. As we went by, they raised their champagne glasses in salute.

Dinner for us was soup and sandwiches, eaten hunkered around a sandy picnic table at a desert campsite. Afterward, a few stayed for the beer and raunchy jokes that Margriet, the Danish horse-trainer, can tell without blushing, although most have already gone to the bathhouse, or to sleep in the musty smelling tents and in sleeping bags out under the stars.

It is still early, and I have walked far enough from camp for the desert to become itself again, stretching away silently forever. It is a good place to think about tomorrow, about going back to Uluru, the Aboriginal sacred site—and tourist attraction. The hundreds, even thousands, of people who emerged from the dunes just after sunset will probably be there, too.

My prayer is for a chance to find a private spot for contemplation. When I close my eyes, I have a vision of looking at the base of Uluru from a little distance, surrounded by water.

FEBRUARY 21, 1997

A<small>T DAWN, OUR GROUP HAD ALREADY PACKED UP AND WAS ON</small> the way back to Uluru.

"Do you know where I was?" I asked Shane, our tour guide, telling him about what I had envisioned. "The water was like a mirror."

"No," he said, and added, "There has been a lot of rain."

Shane has a lot of respect for the land and the Aboriginal people. He was careful to let us know that although visitors can climb to the top of Uluru, the Anangu, the traditional custodians, prefer that we don't. The way up is sacred for them, a path used only by those chosen to mark the beginning of ceremony.

As what I had seen last night was from ground level and not a panoramic view from Uluru's crest, I was one of four who decided to walk around the base. The climbers got off the bus, and as the walkers were being driven in the direction of the Base Walk trailhead, I looked back to watch the others begin their ascent. Truthfully, I was expecting to feel some judgment that so many of our group had chosen not to respect the request of the Anangu. To my surprise, what I saw was the beginning of sacred ceremony, in the way that it has always begun here, with a few members of the clan making the hike to the top.

So early in the morning the Base Walk lay quietly, a flat, well-marked meander in the shadow of Uluru, which rose straight up from the desert floor on our left, its deep red sides gouged by the marks of mythological warfare. In Tjukurpa, Aboriginal Lore, opposing forces met at Uluru. They were the Kuniya, the Rock Python people, and the Liru, the Poisonous Snake Warriors. Their great battles mark the end of the Dreamtime and the beginning of our own age.

The path curved right, around a high flat rock, on whose other side was a shallow salt-pan lake of rainwater. "Here it is!" I said to Shane and the others.

I found the way to climb up and sit sheltered and comfortably on the top of the rock where I could look at the base of Uluru across the little shining lake, its glossy surface burnished with Uluru's reflection. Occasionally I could hear the voices of people walking on the path just below me. They couldn't see me and I couldn't see them. Uluru glowed in front of me, sacred and majestic.

It was beautiful to watch the world wake up and the desert fill with light, and to listen to Uluru begin its hum. The troughs and gullies in the sides of Uluru were the shapes of eagles and snake warriors. In thanks for being where I was, I offered something from my heart and from all the different spiritual traditions I had studied over the years—a Cherokee song of greeting to the beginning of a new day, the Christian hymn "For the Beauty of the Earth," silence, a prayer for peace, a prayer for life, and a Buddhist dedication of merit that my presence at Uluru be for the benefit of all.

When I arrived back at the bus, everyone else was already there, hanging out of the windows with impatience. Shane gave me a thumbs-up.

THE NEXT STOP WAS THE ULURU-KATA TJUTA CULTURAL CENTER, a fabulously organic looking structure with undulating walls and a roof that looks lashed together, like native shelter. At the information desk in a big, high-ceilinged room full of displays, I read that the rock where I had sat at the foot of Uluru is called the Women's Rock and was the initial resting place of the first female Kuniya to arrive there after a long journey from the Dreamtime. She brought her eggs with her by stringing them together and wearing them around her neck, which added to her weariness.

Nearby was a wall of photographs of the park's Boards of Directors. Their smiling faces were both black and white, suggesting that traditional custodians had a say in the governance of the parks. A nearby notice mentioned that while the Anangu do not like to have their picture taken in general, it is particularly against their tradition to display likenesses of the deceased. Here and there, some of the faces had been covered up by little squares of cardboard and black tape, in what appeared to be the compromise that allowed the Anangu to honor their own culture while participating in another.

There was a door right next to the information desk that led to an enclosed courtyard at the center of the building. The courtyard looked innocent enough from what I could see of it through the windows. I went out and sat for awhile eating ice cream on one of the benches away from the crowds. When I was ready to go back in, I couldn't find the door that led to the room I had just left. There were several doors.

Perplexed, I opened and closed each one, then looked around and saw others who, like me, were going from door to door, opening them, shrugging their shoulders, closing them again. There weren't any children doing this. It was an adult experience. Then a man wearing cameras and a striped T-shirt disappeared through a hidden gap in the courtyard wall. The rest of us followed, escaping around the trash dumpsters near a service entrance into the parking lot.

"What was that all about?" an American voice said, as we scurried around the serpentine walls to the front entrance.

"Functional architecture," came an answer from somewhere behind me.

"The Dreamtime," said someone else.

"Usually I enter through the back door," I mused out loud, "and this time I left by it. Things in Australia are upside down or opposite from what I am used to."

AFTER ULURU, OUR TOUR GROUP SPENT THE AFTERNOON AT NEARBY King's Canyon climbing around the fantasically stratified rock that forms it. Then all of us stretched out together on a big tarp under this furthermost sky, for one more night in the desert.

Somebody began to snore and somebody else was throwing shoes, trying to make it stop. The beaming maternal eye of a full moon had begun to rise. I was awake and staring back, wondering about the rest of my trip across Australia.

A large orange planet (was it Mars?) was on fire near the horizon, and a little higher and to the right was the Southern Cross, all its points clear and bright, the celestial "X" that marks due south. I lay there wishing for a constellation that could guide me so precisely to Lorraine Mafi-Williams. I wished for the comfort of a map.

From here on, I was on a choose-my-own-adventure journey, with unconventional means the only "logical" choice to find the way.

FEBRUARY 22, 1997

I HAVE JUST RETURNED TO MY ROOM, AT THE END OF MY LAST DAY in Alice Springs, from dancing at midnight in a crowd being taped for a video. The video stars were an all-Aboriginal rock band. We dancers were of every age and color.

Maybe the music has healed me, because I am feeling better about being here. Tomorrow I fly to Cairns, on the North Queensland coast near the Great Barrier Reef. A friend back home had told me there is a great place to stay a little north of Cairns, on Trinity Beach.

FEBRUARY 24, 1997

Hot! HOT! THE AIR HAS THE CONSISTENCY OF BROTH. The sea is tepid and heaving, as green and dense as algae. It slaps indifferently at the shoreline and is so full of lethal box jellyfish that swimming is restricted to a small, netted area just off the beach.

The motel where I am staying in Trinity Beach has units shaped like igloos, which makes me laugh and doesn't help with the weather. There are only a few other tourists here. I spent the day at a picnic table, drawing palm trees.

FEBRUARY 25, 1997

I HAD A DREAM THAT I WAS TRYING TO CUT A SPIRIT CORD USING a large stone, a kind of crystal. I have never seen one like it before.

The stone was double terminated and radiant, a golden peachy color. The spirit cord was connected on one end directly to the Earth and, on the other, to an Aboriginal man whose image was covered by a small black square, like the ones on the photographs at Uluru.

FEBRUARY 27, 1997

I SPENT TWO EASY DAYS IN THE DAINTREE RAINFOREST AT P.K.'s Jungle Village, talking to Bernard, from Manchester, England. Since then, Far North Queensland feels less than a little lizardy claw's worth of connected to the big Goanna shaping the rest of my trip. It is not the place, it's not the heat. It would be okay if I knew the reason to stay.

To pass the time, I thought it would be fun to scuba dive and signed up for a diving course, only to quit two days later when the instructor remarked that, at average diving depth on the Great Barrier Reef (about sixty feet), there is not enough light to see color. It was as if, suddenly, I remembered that I love to snorkel.

FEBRUARY 28, 1997

MAYBE I AM HERE TO DREAM.

Last night, I dreamed that I walked into a room that was empty except for a dark-skinned man who closed the door behind me.

"Am I the only one who is coming in?" I asked, and he said, "You are the only one who wants to."

It was dark. It was the Dreamtime. I was part of the Dreamtime.

Standing behind me, the man began to remove my skin, starting at my feet and pulling it up in one piece, like something I was wearing. When I looked, I was still "dressed" to the waist. From the waist down, I was a skeleton.

This morning, I slipped on some algae left by high tide, smashing my knee and hitting my head on a rock. Funny thing, I saw the slime and stepped on it anyway.

Sitting there rubbing my forehead and wiping the blood off my leg, I remembered a line from Carol Anthony's *A Guide to the I Ching*—"Unpleasant events serve to jar our minds, telling us that we are on the wrong path."

This isn't the adventure I was looking for. I hobbled back to the motel to book a flight, and tomorrow I leave for Brisbane and Bundjalung country.

MARCH 1, 1997

THE DISTANCE FROM TRINITY BEACH TO BYRON BAY WAS A short flight along the eastern coastline between Cairns and Brisbane, a tolerable layover at the Brisbane transportation terminal and, in the evening, a three-hour bus ride southward.

Beyond the glaring Gold Coast bubble of casinos, nightclubs and hotels, as the two-lane road wound its way through a peaceful rural darkness, I felt a surge, like a mild electrical charge. It was a little nudge, I think, to let me know that I was now in Bundjalung country.

The bus wooshed to a stop in Byron Bay and opened its doors on a roar of people celebrating Friday night. Lights and music blasted from restaurants nearby. For the other passengers on the bus, this must have been what they had come for. Faces expectant, eyes scanning, they rushed to get their backpacks and vanished with a whoop into the swirl.

What I felt was alarm. I walked away from the bus to look for a ride to the motel, forgetting that I had luggage until the taxicab driver asked me for it.

March 2, 1997

I SAT THROUGH MY FIRST MORNING IN BYRON BAY SIGHING happily on the beach, alternately reading and people watching. This afternoon, I went to find Lorraine.

Byron Bay is a pretty resort town, with expensive shops and restaurants, and not where I would have imagined myself looking for an Aboriginal elder. So I wasn't surprised that the man at the Tourist Information office didn't know her. He also told me that there were no sacred Aboriginal sites near Byron Bay; for that I would have to go to the desert.

The young, long-haired volunteer at the Environmental Center knew of several sacred female sites along the coast. He had never heard of Lorraine, so suggested I ask at the Aboriginal Cultural Center. The man at the Cultural Center said, yes, he did know Lorraine, although he didn't know how to reach her and he hadn't seen her for a good while. He was willing to give her a message on how to reach me in case she came by.

After that, I headed back to the beach. What else was there to do? I had traveled fifteen thousand miles, had had a wonderful adventure getting this far, and had given the finding of Lorraine Mafi-Williams my best shot.

"It's time to turn it over," I told myself, and went for a walk along the shoreline to Byron Point, following a well-tended path up to the lighthouse and a clear view of the sea.

There was a wonderful wind blowing, pushing puffball clouds across the summer sky and ruffling the ocean swell into little whitecaps. For the first time I could see the beach on the south side of the point, how it stretched for miles, as curiously empty of people as the town beach on the other side was crowded.

A pair of sea eagles flew by going south, then circled back around and flew south again along the coast. A small pod of dolphins suddenly appeared, swimming in the same direction.

I decided to go south, too, to a place called Suffolk Park and the Sunaway Motel that someone in Trinity Beach had told me about.

I would rent a car. If I wasn't to meet Lorrraine Mafi-Williams, I could spend the week visiting sacred sites, like Mt. Wollumbin and the female areas that I had learned about. I could lie in the sun. I was fine with that.

A FEW HOURS LATER, I FOUND A SCRAP OF WHITE PAPER TAPED TO THE stained glass whale on my motel room door. It was a message from Lorraine, with a friend's telephone number to call for directions on how to find her. I called the number and the friend told me she was living in Suffolk Park.

Everything around me has flashed white.

I think I'm in shock.

Definitely. I'm in shock.

MONDAY

A<small>FTER A BRIEF STOP AT THE</small> S<small>UNAWAY</small> M<small>OTEL</small>, I <small>FOLLOWED</small>
the directions to Lorraine's, winding along a wide road
past hundreds of little treeless yards and look-alike stucco
houses in a housing estate. At the furthest end of the development
the land rose, forming itself into a grassy, treeless ridge that sun-
shimmered along the horizon to end abruptly on its right in a
precipitously high bluff.

Lorraine is staying with her son and his family in a sunbaked
brown-and-tan, one-story duplex. While the middle-aged Aboriginal
man who answered the door went to find her, I waited in the scant
shade under a porch awning and watched the curtained shadows of
two men and a small child moving around in the room beyond the
front window.

Then Lorraine came out and shook my hand and invited me
to sit down outside with her in lawn chairs. We sat facing a bed of

brilliant red flowers that were growing along an unpainted fence.

In the photo in Steven McFadden's book, Lorraine Mafi-Williams looks large, and as steely-eyed as a warrioress, so I wasn't prepared for how small she actually is, just slightly over five feet tall and not very big around. She is also very friendly.

She was wearing a flowered knit dress and was barefoot, so I could see that the two smallest toes on her left foot were partially gone, the same two toes that I had dreamed about that night on the train. "The toes know," I thought. "I've made it to where I am supposed to be."

Lorraine told me that she had come back to Byron Bay just two days before, from Sydney, where she had been ill with kidney problems and in the hospital. She hadn't wanted to come. Her guidance, whom she calls The Band, said that she had to.

She told me that she hadn't really wanted to answer my note, either, and the Band told her she had to do that, too.

"What would you like to do while you are here?" she asked me.

"I'd like to go to Mount Wollumbin," I answered.

"That would be good," she said. "I am the custodian for Wollumbin. I've been away for six months and need to go there, although now I don't have a car."

"Well, I do," I said happily.

To get out of the sun, we moved to sit on a sofa stored in the one-car garage, and Lorraine began to tell me stories, some of them traditional ones that were already familiar. An hour or so went by. I was delighted that she was willing to spend so much time with me.

Her daughter-in-law Sylvia came to say that she was leaving to see her husband, Dean, Lorraine's son, who was in the hospital with an infected leg. Two willowy young girls got off a school bus and ran toward the house and I got up to leave, arranging to come back in the morning for the ride to Wollumbin.

Before going, I gave Lorraine the two shirts I had brought from Nashville. She said her grandchildren would love the one with the frog on it. I told her where it had come from. I said I had seen the Harley-Davidson T-shirt in the same meditation, and I didn't know any more about it.

"Well, then," she said politely.

As I was getting in the car, I asked Lorraine if the beautiful, shimmering hill behind the housing estate was special to her people. Yes, she said; the story was very sad, and she wouldn't want me to have to share that kind of sadness.

I felt sad anyway, at the idea of seeing something so peaceful and lovely every day and remembering a story that was too sad to tell.

THE SUNAWAY MOTEL CLAIMS TO BE THE MOST EASTERLY MOTEL IN Australia. It sits tucked away on the last of a cluster of residential streets, behind the Suffolk Park Post Office. The motel is a short row of 1960s shotgun-style units—each with a kitchen, bedroom, bath and a sunporch on the end. It is separated by a jungly strip of trees and bushes from the house next door, and has the smallest pool I have ever seen.

This afternoon, I crossed the little road to follow a public foot-path through the dunes and sea grass and walked out onto the sand in the very middle of the same stretch of deserted coastline I had seen from Byron Point. What a blessing of sun and solitude! There wasn't a house or hotel in sight, and the only people were a few tiny specks near the lighthouse at the beach's northern end. Far to the south was Broken Head, where Lorraine said there was easy access to the Taylor Lakes, one of the local female sacred sites I had learned about.

I stayed on the beach until after dark and the softest wind had scattered the stars across the mirroring sea, as still as glass at low tide. Just as I turned to go, the large orange planet I had seen in the desert (was it Mars?) rose above the rim of the world and glowed like flame across the water.

Later in the evening, I answered the knock at my door and there was Lorraine. Could she come in? Please! Would you like something to drink? Yes, please! We retreated to the sun porch.

On the sun porch daybed was Steven McFadden's book *Ancient Voices, Current Affairs*—as it turned out, the first finished copy Lorraine had seen. She was delighted to discover that she was Chapter Eight (a sacred number for her), and was surprised into silence by her photograph.

After some moments, she smiled shyly and said, "My, I do look fierce, don't I?" Apparently it had been her Band's idea to paint on the white dots, something she had never done before.

Just outside, the wind advanced and withdrew, clacking the palm leaves with the rhythm of the sea tides. Inside we drank tea, ate candy bars and smoked. For the first time, I was feeling not quite so guilty about smoking again. Maybe a greater purpose was being served.

I asked Lorraine if she knew which planet was the orange one, and she told me a story about smoking!

AN ELDER SHE KNEW WAS TEACHING HIS TRADITIONAL WISDOM TO a group of whites, and one of the young men in the group kept commenting on the fact that the old teacher smoked. He kept saying over and over, "I can't believe you smoke."

One night the young man said, "What do you call that?" and pointed to the planet glowing large and orange on the horizon.

The elder said, "That is God, and he is smoking a cigar."

LORRAINE WAS SITTING IN A RATTAN ARMCHAIR, AND I SHIFTED FROM pillows on the floor to the daybed to the floor again while she told stories and I listened. Occasionally I asked a question, which would always lead to another story (of all kinds, traditional ones, ones I call planetary wisdom, and more personal ones about her life). This evening I had my journal handy to make notes as quick as I could.

I liked the way Lorraine laughed a lot when her own stories got funny. She had been told by a Hopi elder that she has Heyokah medicine.

ORIGINS ......

OUR OLD PEOPLE TELL US THAT WE ORIGINALLY CAME FROM A PLANET THAT HAD SEEN ITS TIME AND BLEW UP.

It was the 10th planet in this solar system. Our people went and lived in the Pleiades for a while, and then we were asked to come to Earth to help create and maintain the grid system because we knew about that from our own planet.

The grid system is a grid of energy that helps protect the planet as it undergoes its changes. It helps the Earth maintain balance. We call this system Boamie, the Rainbow Serpent. It has all the colors of the rainbow—the colors of the jewels, which are female, and the minerals, which are male; all the substances buried in the Earth's crust that keep the grid system strong.

Our old people know how to call up the rainbows so they can check the health of the grid system, so they see where the system needs work. An incomplete rainbow is a sign of illness.

The eleventh planet, it is disintegrating and will be gone in another thousand years or so. It is the source of all the shooting stars that we see. The gravity of this planet is so powerful that we are pulled toward it, not the shooting stars toward us. The inhabitants of this planet have been reincarnating here for a few thousand years. I have met three of them — two in Australia, one in the U.S. I felt humbled by them. They are so radiant.

The twelfth planet is the home of the Federation of Twelve and goes wherever it wants to.

OTHER RACES

THE ANASAZI CAME FROM THE SAME PLANET AS THE ABORIGINES.

The Aborigine's job was to maintain the grid system. The Anasazi's job was to raise the food for the generations to come. I was shown this by an old Native American man in gold buckskins who came to me in a vision when I was in New Mexico. In the vision, I saw a sea of corn stretching away to the horizon. The Anasazi grew tired of the wickedness on the Earth and went back to the stars.

The Adnyamathanha people of the Flinders Ranges were not the same as other Aboriginal people; they were of a different race. They were called the People Kept Apart, not to isolate them, but for protection. They were the keepers of Lemurian knowledge, and their center was Wilpena Pound.

THE SUN AND THE MOON

THE MOON MOVES THE NINE PLANETS ANTI-CLOCKWISE.

The Sun is manmade. One of the ancient civilizations who worshipped the Sun, the Incans or the Aztecs or the Mayans, made the Sun. They made the Sun out of a big disc of gold and uranium and took it through a portal to the center of the earth and to the circle of fire that is in the center of the earth. And when they got near the fire, which is solar, it pushed it back up, right up into the heavens.

One of the planets, the fiery planet Jupiter, which we call Narla, gives the energy to one side of the Sun, and the fire energy from Earth, which is coupled with Moon energy, heats the other side. The energy that comes back to Earth from the Sun is a nice combination of solar and Moon energy. Our bodies receive this Moon and Sun energy, with the hot-blooded men receiving the solar energy and the women receiving the Moon. There has to be that perfect balance all the time.

The Moon is in the center of the universe, and it moves the planets around anti-clockwise. The fiery planet Jupiter moves the Sun clockwise. During an eclipse, when the Moon and the Sun meet, there is a perfect balance of solar and Moon energy, and that is what we get.

Women receive both energies through the blood and the water in their bodies. And as the Moon controls water and the tides, so it controls the fluids in the women's bodies. When we women receive the Moon energy, it comes down through our hair, our hair receiving like an antenna. We bring it down through the right side of our body and we put that Moon energy into the earth. The men receive the fire, Jupiter's fiery solar energy, up their left side and they shoot that energy up to the Sun through the top of their head. The energy goes in a perfect circle.

The Above depends on us to look after the Below. We human beings are the only connection from up there to the Earth. We need to be in balance, so we can put that energy from the Moon or the Sun into the Earth. And if we are in balance, not too much male or too much female, this will keep the Mother Earth in balance and keep us in balance, and that keeps everything else in balance, in perfect harmony, and coordination and rhythm and balance.

We are receptors. That's why we human beings were

put on this Earth. When people say that human beings will become extinct, I say, "No, we create. The Earth itself and the animals and the birds and the beasts, they become extinct because they evolve. Humanity does not evolve. We create."

That is where a lot of scientists and historians go wrong, too. They have it back to front. They think we evolve like animals evolve, but we don't. We create. We are recreated all the time.

CAN I HAVE YOUR HOUSE?

I WAS ASKED TO SPEAK TO THIS GROUP OVER IN NORTH SYDNEY, AND NORTH SYDNEY IS LIKE MANHATTAN, FULL OF MANSIONS AND PEOPLE DRIVING AROUND IN ROLLS ROYCES AND BMWs.

So I was asked to go over there, and the group was more concerned and worried about the predictions, the environmental predictions, like tidal waves and earthquakes and things like that.

Well, Australia has never had major earthquakes yet. We have had earth tremors and things like that, but nothing really big, and our old people say that when there is a wave, it will be not so much a tidal wave from the sea, but waves of disease, waves of famine, waves of what humanity causes, and not so much the elements.

There were lots of predictions going around about fifteen years ago about one half of Sydney was going to be washed away, and there were going to be big earthquakes and people should start looking for safe places. So when I went over to talk to this group, they were all in a panic and wanting to know how to look after their business or whether their business was going to fold, the stock markets and things like that.

And I said, "Yes, our old people said there is going to be three major stock market drops. We have had two. There is one more to come, and that is the one that will wipe money and all that sort of stuff out."

So anyway, when I went over to this place, oh, this house was a beautiful, big mansion, chandeliers all over the place and statues and heroines' busts. The lady who was the hostess, she was wearing diamonds and furs. So I spoke for about two hours or something like that, and I was reassuring the people that there was no need to panic or run away.

Everyone was talking about moving into the Blue Mountains, just outside of Sydney here. They were all going to pack up and go and live in the mountains. And I said, "What if the earthquake hits the Blue Mountains? What are you going to do then?"

That brought them back to reality. But this lady was

still persistent and still making plans to go and live here and live there, and by the end of the session this lady, the hostess, was still saying to me, "Oh, I think I should build a house and go and live in the mountains."

By that time I was tired of talking and explaining, so I said to her, "Okay, you go live in the Blue Mountains. Can I have your house?"

Well, you could have heard a pin drop. Goodness me, Aboriginals moving to the North Shore. There goes the neighborhood.

THE PREDICTIONS FROM OUR OLD PEOPLE WERE MORE OR LESS THE SAME AS WHAT MEDIUMS AND PROPHETS WERE SAYING.

But our predictions were much more on a practical level. Like the old people were saying, "Yes, there are going to be waves, but not water." Waves of murder and disease like AIDS and things like that, waves of crimes, what humanity brings on itself. There have been natural disasters around the world, earthquakes and floods. Look at India.

In the United States, I asked especially for someone to take me to see the San Andreas Fault. I had a look at that. That is going to close when the shift starts, because the earth is rotating on an axis and at the moment it is going really fast, and then boom, it is going to drop, and then some of the continent is going to be missing. I don't know where.

And when it tilts, up will rise the remains of Lemuria and the earth will jam together very quickly and it will close that fault.

We don't know when that shift is going to happen. But it won't be traumatic. We might not feel it. We won't feel it. They may feel it up in Canada or Alaska, up in the top there where it is moving very quickly, that axis, but we here in Australia won't feel it very much.

But we will know when the shift occurs. And everybody will know, because all of a sudden, there will be a new bit of landscape to appear, or the fault line will start to close.

The Earth will come back into its proper balance and spin slowly like it used to. You might have noticed that when you were a child the days seemed so long and summer was actually summer and winter was actually winter, but now we are having rain here in summer when it doesn't normally rain. That has got to do with the elements' changes.

A year goes very quick, because the Earth is spinning toward its final shift and then back to normal. And we won't feel it. And everyone is packing up to go and live in different places.

I am staying put in my little house. The shifts have been occurring for the last fifty or sixty years. Nothing to get all panicky about, because the Twelve up there, they have got the hands in control of old mother Earth here, and they are not going to let it go.

ALL OUR TEACHERS COME FROM ABOVE.

There are the Planetary Beings, that we call our friends, the Twelve, the Confederation, and all the other ones on the different planets and star people. We still get the teachings from them direct, down to the Spirit Ancestors, who then teach it to the living, to the living teachers, who translate it into our understanding and we put it out.

That is how our system is.

NEAR MIDNIGHT, AS I DROVE LORRAINE HOME, SHE ASKED ME IF I had felt comfortable in Byron Bay.

"Not much," I answered. "I thought it was because it was a party town."

She told me that the town is built in a traditional men's area, a place where a woman can go, even live, but will never feel the spaciousness of truly being at home there.

TUESDAY

I WAS AT LORRAINE'S HOUSE AT 10 A.M. THIS MORNING FOR OUR trip to Wollumbin. With her son in the hospital, I am still both mystified and gratified by the amount of time Lorraine has for spending with me, away from her family. Of course, I know this trip today is about her role as a custodian, and I am the one with the car.

We were stopped in Byron Bay, for cigarettes and cold drinks and a visit to the post office, when Lorraine said to me, "Do you have a tape recorder?" and I said, "Let me see what I can do."

The Byron Bay electronics store was closed, so, on a chance, I walked across the street to the Environmental Center and asked the pleasant, middle-aged man behind the desk if he happened to have one he could lend me.

"I know this is a strange request," I told him. "I'm hoping to tape the stories of an Aboriginal elder."

As he was smiling and shaking his head "no," the woman behind him reached under the counter and pulled a tape recorder out of her handbag.

"I lent this to a friend of mine months ago," she said, "and she just gave it back to me this morning."

She handed it to me and looked amazed.

So Lorraine and I were off, away from the coast and heading for Wollumbin, Mount Warning, by way of Nimbin, a community in the hills a little to the south. The day was beautiful, breezy and not too hot, and the countryside was lush and green from a lot of rain.

Lorraine commented that New South Wales never used to get so much rain this time of year. Things were different now. In the old days, she said, the weather was in perfect balance. There was lots of sunshine, but when rain was needed, there were those who knew how to call for it, with prayer and ceremony, and it would come. Just enough, never more. Now there was too much rain, or it was too dry.

As we drove, I asked Lorraine questions about her life. How, for instance, did her mother and father meet? I knew from Steven McFadden's book that they were of different clans and different areas.

Later on, she told me a funny story about her mentor and teacher Mrs. Millie Boyd, an elder and clan relation of Lorraine's husband, who was of the Githrabaul people.

MARRIAGE AND LORE vs. LAW

OUR CUSTOM BEFORE, AND THERE ARE PARTS OF AUSTRALIA WHERE THE CUSTOM IS STILL CARRIED OUT, WAS ARRANGED MARRIAGES.

Now the reason why a lot of our marriages were arranged by our parents and our grandparents is because the clans are so close, we didn't want to be intermarrying with our own tribal people. So wives and husbands were chosen from other countries and other clans and other tribes, to keep our bloodline pure.

And see, it was always our custom, and still is today, that the women follow their mother's and their grandmother's lineage. They don't adopt the husband's. The boys take their father's and their grandfather's lineage and they do not adopt their mother's customs or language or country or anything, so the two stay completely different, completely different, even the language. But when the children are taught, well, the children learn three dialects, really. So they learn their mother's language and they learn their father's language and they also learn English. So there are the three languages that they learn. Now some of the languages are lost. There is not so much language left. But we still teach the children the culture and the old customs as much as we possibly can, because once the children learn English and go to school, then they adopt a lot of white ways. We have to live by white ways, what with integration and government policy and all that sort of thing, so we are holding very hard to our customs that are left and our traditions that are left.

White society's got the impression that our language, culture, Lore, and history, and everything, is gone and dead. And it is not. We just keep it to ourselves and keep it underground and we practice it at home. See, if I didn't know any of the language, the Lore, the customs, or where our ceremonial sites are, where the men's ground is, the women's ground is, I wouldn't be taking Anne on a journey like this. I wouldn't know how to do it. So I am living proof that we do still carry our culture and our Lore.

It is L-o-r-e, not like white man's L-a-w. We have to live by white man's Law, but we have to observe and obey our old traditional Lore and customs. And our Lore goes right back for thousands and thousands of years, whereas the white lore, the English Law, is changing all the time. No sooner do we get used to one white Law, than it changes. The government will change the police or the legal system, or the judicial system will change and then we're none the wiser for the White man's Law. And because we can't keep up with the changes in the judicial system or the legal system, we get in a lot of trouble about that.

ELVIS

AUNT MILLIE WAS A GREAT FAN OF ELVIS PRESLEY.

Ahh, she had all sorts of souvenirs of Elvis, things like plates and cups and flags, a lot of different things.

Auntie Millie asked me to make a little film called *Eelemarni,* which is her tribal name. And after I had finished the filming and editing, it came time to add the music. Would you believe that Auntie Millie said, "I want Elvis singing 'Blue Suede Shoes?'"

The story of *Eelemarni* is two to three thousand years old. So I replied, "Auntie Millie, you can't have Elvis singing 'Blue Suede Shoes' to an ancient traditional story; it would wreck it. Didgeridoo music would be more appropriate."

And she replied, "I am not going to act any more or say anymore if you don't have Elvis playing 'Blue Suede

Shoes.'"

I worked it out by adding a scene to the film where Auntie Millie says that the legendary figure being depicted was as famous in his day as Elvis Presley was in present time. That is how I got Auntie Millie to finish the project.

THERE WAS A PARTICULAR PLACE ALONG THE TREE-LINED ROADS AS we headed to Nimbin that Lorraine leaned forward in the seat, tape recorder running, and began a conversation with the guardians of the land.

PERMISSION

I WILL SHOW A POINT WHERE THE SPIRITS
WILL BE STARTING TO LOOK AT US
AND IT'S OKAY, BECAUSE THE SPIRITS
ARE OF MY ANCESTORS ON MY FATHER'S SIDE,
BECAUSE THIS IS MY FATHER'S COUNTRY HERE.

This is Bundjalung country up this way. And I will show you the point where they will start watching us. And when they see that you are with me, or I am with you, it will be all right for you to come here tomorrow on your own. But I must bring you through first. This is my way of introducing you to my ancestor spirits that look after these places around here, near Nimbin.

And I don't have to call out loud and say, "This is Anne from America. She is my friend. It's okay. Well, can she look around a bit?" I don't have to say that, I only have to speak that to my mind, in my mind, because our people still use telepathy. They will read my thoughts through telepathy.

And if I want to listen to what they want to say, it is on the wind, in the breeze, and they will tell me if I am not welcome, or if Anne is not welcome, or anybody else is not welcome, and that's the way that I will know if I should not bring anybody into parts of Nimbin.

But so far, so good, and there is no sign of the spirits disagreeing with me taking Anne in now.

See that big rock over there? Well, it comes down toward the road, that's where our ancestors will be waiting and looking and watching us now. They are sitting up there now. So, if they didn't want me to take you or anybody through into Nimbin, they would give me signs, they'd speak to me in telepathy. And they haven't yet, so that is good.

I will ask you to come from Byron Bay up to Lismore and from Lismore out here, for two reasons. It's better to enter from the West, for us, for our people, and it is also a better road and it's quicker. We have done a complete half-circle, we have come the long way around.

Up a narrow, twisty, bumpy road we went, and suddenly there we were on Nimbin's Main Street. The buildings' fronts were painted with rainbows, there were people wearing tie-dye clothes, and pot was for sale on the sidewalks. It was startling, like waking up from a dream about the 1990s still in the '60s and the Summer of Love.

Nimbin is in Bundjalung country, and Lorraine seemed happy and comfortable there. She was recognized as we walked in and out of shops, and she said that Nimbinites were always ready to activate themselves in support of Aboriginal Rights.

Unlike other places I had visited in Australia, here dark-skinned and white-skinned people appeared to be living equally on the same piece of ground.

We went to the Nimbin Museum, which houses a collection of litter and kitsch glued together into outrageous social commentaries. As we strolled through the series of tiny windowless rooms, the museum's sound system was playing Nawang Khechog, a Tibetan flute player. Lorraine said her Band had led her to his door one evening in Sydney, to ask for permission to use his music as a movie soundtrack for *Eelemarni*. I told her that once in an auditorium in Indiana, where I had gone with a group of friends to see the Dalai Lama, I had burst into tears at the sound of Nawang Khechog's Universal Horn.

Back in the car, we drove out the other side of Nimbin. Main Street turned back into a winding two-lane road and took us to Nimbin Rocks, the Aboriginal sacred site that gives the area its name. I was glad for the privilege of going there with Lorraine. The Rocks were imposing-looking, but not monumental. Without her, I might have driven by without a second glance.

Standing on the side of the road with her, listening to her describe the importance of Nimbin Rocks, I could feel again the fragmentation that can occur when two cultures collide. The original people of Australia find spirtual significance in natural formations, in the land itself. Their way is to honor it and leave it alone. The Europeans who settled the lovely sweep of valley around Nimbin Rocks were more accustomed to saying their prayers indoors. They came to own the land and fenced it in for crops and livestock.

NIMBIN

THIS IS NIMBIN, THESE ROCKS OUT HERE.

Actually Nimbin is the English name. We call it Nyimbunji. They couldn't say that, the English.

So Nyimbunji is where only the very, very high medicine men used to teach the younger men who were seeking higher visions to be a high magician, or shaman, or somebody high up in rank. They used to come from all over Australia to be taught here.

The young men learned where the energy from the crystal and ley line grids was, so that the energy would fill their bodies and they were able to levitate or fly as we say — levitate in the wind, traveling the wind. Their feet were never to touch the ground.

And because they were so high up in magic, they could find portals underneath the ground and travel from one end of the country to the other in ten minutes. Well, this is where they were taught that, just here. They would have to jump from that rock right down to the flat, levitate or fly down, and that was very high magic. And this is the only place where it used to be taught. From all parts of Australia, they would come here.

There are actually three rocks, three pinnacles, that have English names. As this is men's area and men's country and men's mountain, I don't know the men's name for them, because I am a woman. I am really an outsider as well, even though this is my dad's country. We are safe here in my dad's country, but as I am a woman, I don't press my luck, so the spirits won't chastise me.

The English call one of the pinnacles Needle Rock. And the little rock jumping out, that looks like the face of a little elf or a deva or little being, well, that is Nyimbunji. Can you see his little face? He is a little fellow. He comes from around here. We see him sometimes. That is where he lives, in that rock. And that rock behind, see that Aboriginal face at the back? That's the Old Man, that one.

Little Nyimbunji, he is like the little deva, and he is about two feet tall. He's like a little leprechaun. "Nyimbunji" simply means "home" or "house." That was what Nimbin was supposed to be called.

There was some confusion about which was the way to Wollumbin, but eventually we found it, a tiny road that went by a campground on the left before starting to wind its way up the mountain. Around a steep curve was a peeling motel sign, and Lorraine said "Turn here."

We drove along a gravel driveway, past a wooden building of motel-style rooms that looked shabby and neglected. There was a tennis court with weeds fanning out from the cracks in the surface, a small pool that looked clean and used, a dining hall and a caretaker's house, obviously lived in. Behind the buildings were unmown fields and a lake.

Lorraine was saying that several years ago, she and Aunt Millie had been invited here to a workshop and ceremonies organized by two American women and Biannca Pace, her friend in Sydney. A few weeks before the workshop, as the story goes, a wealthy man touring the countryside on a motorcycle had fallen in love with the area and bought the motel. From the look of things, not much was being done with it.

Lorraine glanced around at the unkempt grounds and sighed. She had always wanted to have a place like this, out in the country. Her dream was to set up a cultural center and reconnect Aboriginal children living in cities to the land and their ancient traditions. She couldn't believe that the person who had bought the motel was letting it go to waste.

"Why don't you go knock on the door and ask the caretaker if this place is being used for anything?" I suggested, pulling the car into the turnaround in front of the house. "If it is not, it might be an opportunity. Maybe the owner would be interested in sponsoring a cultural center, too."

She told me that it wouldn't do for an Aboriginal woman to go knocking on strange doors and asking questions like that. So I said, "OK, I'll do it."

No one was home.

BACK OUT ON THE MOUNTAIN ROAD, WE CROSSED A STREAM AND SAW another driveway next to a sign with the words *Sri Sathya Sai* on it. Sai, as in Sai Baba? I remembered that Suzee had said to me before leaving Nashville to keep Sai Baba in mind.

"Do you know what that is?" I asked Lorraine.

She thought it was a religious community of some sort, on land owned by someone famous.

I was starting to turn in, saying, "Maybe we ought to go and see what's there," but Lorraine wanted to continue on up the mountain. It was getting late and apparently we needed to be gone from Wollumbin before the sun set. "All right," I said, and stayed on the main road, thinking that there would be a chance to come back and find out where this second driveway went.

A short distance further up, the road ended in a small parking lot. Lorraine got out of the car and headed for a picnic table in the shade of Mount Wollumbin's rainforest vegetation, as large-leafed and sheltering as a forest of umbrellas.

Lorraine had been energetic all day, but now sat heavily, leaning sideways on one arm. She lit another cigarette and seemed to expel herself in each outbreath of smoke. For the first time I remembered that she had only been out of the hospital less than a week.

I sat with her, listening to the white noise of the mountain stream nearby, the same one we had crossed earlier. Two enormous dark-feathered birds, with short tails and necks, strutted across the pavement, picking at little piles of picnic litter, clucking expectantly.

Lorraine pointed at the birds and started to fiddle with the tape recorder. "Those are mountain turkeys, she said. "Now I will just tell a little bit about Wollumbin. The English name is Mount Warning."

WOLLUMBIN

NOW WE ARE HERE, AT THE BASE OF WOLLUMBIN, MOUNT WARNING.

Wollumbin means Eagle, Eagle Hawk. This is his home here.

When I was in training with Auntie Mil, no matter whether I was living up around here or working in Sydney, I would go home and pick up Auntie Mil and a change of clothes and blankets and pillows and down at the bottom, at the caravan park, that is where we would camp. We would stay for about a week. This is where Auntie Mil and I would come, and she would give me the teachings.

She never actually climbed the mountain, but night times she would go on her journey and she would go right up to the top there and check the place out and see if everything was all right and come back. She would have what a lot of people call an out-of-body experience, when your spirit goes and your body is in a bed, but our old people, once we get to that stage in our teachings, they can do that. When I am about sixty-five, then I will know and I will be able to automatically send my spirit wherever I want to go.

So we used to stay down there for about a week, camping in a caravan, and every night, Auntie Mil would go around the area in spirit, not in her physical body.

THEY TELL ME THAT IN THE OLD DAYS
MOUNT WARNING, WOLLUMBIN, USED TO BE
A MOUNTAIN FOR A REALLY HIGH SHAMAN,
AND FOR SUNDANCES,
AND THAT IT BELONGED TO THE
NORTH AMERICAN INDIANS.

No particular tribe owned it. It belonged to all of the men.

This was at a time, thousands and thousands and millions of years ago, when the Earth was one, one big landmass before it split into the continents that it is now. So

Wollumbin belonged to the Indian people. But when the Earth split, the mountain stayed within Australian soil.

Our people in the old days knew about the mountain and they cared for it and looked after it. In 1981 or 1982 or 1983, I am not too sure which year it was, the three old women who had been handed down the responsibility over the years of being the custodians, the caretakers, came and opened it up for National Parks and Wildlife so they could look after it and care for this mountain and people can walk up and down and look at it, a tourist attraction. That was Sister Mary and Mrs. Millie Boyd (Auntie Mil), and another old lady named Auntie Eileen Morgan, who is still alive. We have lost Auntie Mil and we have lost Sister Mary. The three old women opened up this mountain so everyone could come and have a look. Prior to that time, only the caretakers used to come and visit here, to maintain it.

When the big cataclysm happened, there was one particular Indian medicine man that lived on this mountain all the time, and his name was Waugatha. Now I don't know, none of us knew, what actual tribe he belonged to. We don't know that. Now the story of Waugatha is that after many years, he turned into an eagle. There is a big eagle on this mountain, a big golden one, and he doesn't show himself very much. His name is Wollumbin, which means eagle.

Wollumbin is a "Nrrahpul" word.[4] I am not sure how to spell it, but it is the sound of the eagle's war cry. This is the eagle's mountain, and it is the "Nrrahpul" people that live around it.

In the old days, we believed that we got our languages and dialect from the birds, from birdcalls. One day the eagle was fighting with one of the little scrub turkeys that make their nest here. As the eagle drove the turkeys away, he kept screaming his war cry, and the warriors who were walking nearby, said, "Oh, we like that sound. We are going to call our clan the 'Nrrahpul' people."

That is how they got their name from this mountain and this eagle. So that story has been handed down.

Now there could be other tribal people who have custodianship of this mountain, because all the tribes used to come and camp around here and live. And I am not a "Nrrahpul" person, but I married into the Githrabaul tribe, who on the women's side are "Nrrahpul" women. Auntie Mil was a "Nrrahpul" woman, and she handed over all of her responsibilities to me, because I was her student and her apprentice.

I was also taught a lot of the things from my parents and from many elders from different parts. I am now custodian of this mountain.

THERE IS ANOTHER PART TO THE STORY OF THIS MOUNTAIN.

When the earth was one, there was a diamond shape made by four mountains, and each mountain had a really big quartz. Some were clear crystal quartz and some were rosy quartz.

Now in Wollumbin, inside that mountain there, there is a really big activating rosy quartz crystal, and when the Harmonic Convergence energy happened here, that energy spread right through all of the activating points of the energy grid, the crystal grid.

That energy had to come from women, not the men. The men couldn't put that energy into the Earth. Only the women could do that. Although the mountain itself belongs to the men, the women activated this big crystal, a balance of male and female.

I don't mind telling people that in this mountain there is a really big crystal quartz, because they can't chop it up and drag it away and take it home. It is too big, as big as a house, and it is covered by a lot of undergrowth and this beautiful rainforest and dirt. So you can't get to it, but the energy is there, and it is spreading all the time.

LORRAINE CLICKED OFF THE TAPE RECORDER AND WE SAT FOR A while, listening to the sounds of the mountain—the sound of the clear mountain water hissing loudly around the rocks in the streambed—the sound of the mountain turkeys, cackling skittishly around the picnic tables—and the sound of a little mountain breeze rattling the leaves as it waltzed through the forest, dancing with light and shadow.

"Lorraine? Did I tell you about the man who said I would cross an ocean and meet a woman and it would change my life?"

"I don't remember that," she answered.

"When he said it, I didn't know who he was talking about, although in a way I did. I remembered the first time I looked at your photograph in Steven McFadden's book and felt like I was looking at myself."

Lorraine cocked a quizzical look in my direction, and I laughed. It was just the way Alex had looked at me when I had told him the same thing.

"I know. It was strange. I would look at your picture and think, 'Well my eyes are a little that way; and I can stand with my arms crossed, with that don't-mess-with-me look on my face. Maybe that's it.' It's taken me awhile, even up to right now and sitting here with you, to better understand."

I had to stop speaking for a minute. I was getting ready to claim a kinship, and all the reasons why that couldn't possibly be so were making my voice wobble. Lorraine didn't say anything, and I started talking again.

"For one thing, I'm one of the Sacred Sites Group. It's not a formal group, just people with a common interest who get together and visit the ancient Native American sites near where we live. Although we always have somebody along who talks about the site historically, and archaeologically, our main purpose is to honor the Earth with our prayers. Our ceremonies are always just a little different from each other, because they depend on who comes. And we don't all share the same spiritual traditions. Like yours, our intention is always the same. We all want to practice good stewardship of the earth in a sacred way.

"So we come together in a circle, and whoever wants to can

offer a prayer, or a song, or a ritual, or a poem, a reflection of their own particular journey. The offerings come from everywhere, because the people in the circle are from everywhere: Christian, Buddhist, Native American, Jewish, wherever. Somehow it all fits together. It's wonderful, miraculous. It is an experience of wholeness. It's hard to find the words for what happens. You know what I mean?"

I stopped talking and glanced at Lorraine, trying to decide whether to keep going. She had just lit another cigarette and was looking away into the forest, listening to my story pretty much in the same way that I listen to hers—not asking much about it, not fidgeting too much, just listening.

"Lorraine, did I tell you that I have the memory of a planet blowing up, too?'

"I don't think you did," she answered.

"It was not much more than a flash of light and a terrible, terrible feeling. No story to go with it, like you have in your tradition. No way to know where to look or what to look for.

"I had a dream on the way here, one night on the North Queensland coast. I dreamed that I went into a room with an Aboriginal man and he removed my skin from my feet up to my waist. I looked down and all I could see was my skeleton. I didn't remember at the time that a while back, the priest of the church where I was going told me 'If God is our Father, then our Mother is the Church.' I walked around for days after that feeling like a balloon—no legs, no feet, no ground to stand on. Everything above, nothing below. I kept trying to push a belief in what he had said down past my belly button, and it wouldn't go. I hope I have a chance some day to thank him, the priest, I mean. If he hadn't said that, I might never have realized that parts of me were missing.

"I guess there can be a lot of ways to interpret a dream. In mine, everything felt stripped away, down to the foundation. I saw bones, pelvic bones, leg bones and feet bones standing flat on the ground. Maybe it is a good omen for the future. Maybe those good bones have grown from all the ways that I have known myself since the balloon days. Like being with the Sacred Sites group and sitting in circle and learning how to hold the Earth and the things that are important to me sacred. Like having a teacher and mentor like Suzee Waters Benjamin, who has always been willing to go first and show the way, like Aunt Millie did for you. Suzee is the one who brings the music.

"I have had time and opportunities to sit with Buddhist teachers and Native American elders in ceremony, so I could experience right relationship as something more than an idea and know in different ways that 'Oh, is this what it is?' I have had this opportunity to be with you and visit the sacred places that you are custodian for. I think everything's working out all right......Lorraine?

"Yes, Anne?" she said, while gathering up the cigarettes and the tape recorder.

"We both like to write poetry."

WE GOT BACK IN THE CAR AND STARTED DOWN THE MOUNTAIN. Lorraine mentioned she and her sister Elaine were going to Lismore the next day for a session concerning Aboriginal Rights. She was sorry that she wouldn't be able to spend the time with me.

Just then we passed the *Sri Sathya Sai* sign, and I commented that tomorrow might be a good day for me to come back and make a visit to whatever was at the end of that driveway.

"You could climb the trail to the top of Wollumbin," Lorraine added. "That would be a good thing for you to do."

On the way to Byron Bay, we stopped in to say hello to Lorraine's sister, Elaine, who had just moved to a new apartment. Among other things, Lorraine wanted to show me a painting Elaine had that told the story of several women who had been killed and thrown into one of the Taylor Lakes.

The connection between Lorraine and Elaine was so energetic that just being with them together was fun. We laughed a lot, and I took a picture of them, the two sisters arm-in-arm, smiling hugely at each other. Lorraine told Elaine about the motel, and they discussed contacting a local politician they knew who might be able to help.

I saw the painting, a swirl of faces and brown paint, and pretty soon afterward Lorraine and I left.

IT HAD BEEN A LONG DAY, AND NOW THAT I WAS A LITTLE WORRIED about her health, I thought it unlikely that Lorraine would want to have tea with me again. I asked her anyway, and she said yes. We stopped at a bakery in Suffolk Park for a box of pastries and drove on to the Sunaway Motel.

There was a linen cart on the covered walk outside the rooms. As I was nudging my door open, Susie, the owner, walked by and said hello. Lorraine was suddenly nervous, hesitant.

"Is everything OK?" I asked her. I was already in the kitchen and turned around just as Lorraine stepped—actually, she hopped—in behind me and started walking to the sun porch.

"Aborigines have to be careful in this country," she said. "There is a lot of racism. I think that it is all right here."

Lorraine settled back into the rattan armchair. I constructed a cozy pile of throw pillows from the daybed and stretched out on the floor.

We ate, we drank, and Lorraine started telling me stories. Tonight, they made me laugh, infuriated me because of the misuse they documented, and made me sad, all at the same time.

We talked about the "stolen generation," the Aboriginal children whom the Australian government removed from their families and institutionalized, then put to work as domestics for white families.

All five of the children in Lorraine's family were stolen. Lorraine was twelve at the time. Her youngest sister, Elaine, was five. Until the family was finally reunited, when Lorraine was about twenty, she and her siblings and her parents had no contact. They didn't even know each other's whereabouts.

STOLEN

GOSH, THEY WERE REALLY LEARNING TIMES.

We survived it all. It took some doing, but we did it.

And I was told that Indian children, too, were taken

away like we were, but they were put in schools. We weren't. We weren't. We were put in institutions to learn how to look after people's houses, to be housemaids, and the boys were laborers. Never anything that wasn't about being a domestic. We weren't given the opportunity to be nurses or anything. We all had to be able to scrub somebody's floors, or wash their clothes, or look after their children.

And never paid. We were supposed to get money when we turned twenty-one. I remember, they started working me when I was fifteen until I was eighteen (we were allowed to go home when we were eighteen), and all those years I never got paid. None of us got paid, us girls, not even the boys. No. We worked for people for only our bed and feed, that's all. We were supposed to collect money when we were twenty-one, but I remember I only got one-hundred-eighty pounds for all those years I worked, all those years.

Anyway, we survived it. We are better off for it—not the working for nothing--but at least it made us wiser, I think. Look at how people work just for money now. They worship it.

People didn't feel the first stock market crash so much, but a lot of them felt the second one. A lot of them killed themselves, especially the men, because their businesses were just wiped out in an instant. Gee, what will they feel when they have to face the third one, the big one, the final one? That will wipe it all out, nearly all of it.

Oh, my goodness, I hope I'm not filthy rich by then.

I'll put my money in a hollow log or something.

We will all have to get back to the trading days. That will be good. I would rather trade something for food or travel or whatever. I've never had any money. I've got a good tongue. I can share that.

She told me another story, about her Uncle Tommy, who was a linguist for his clan. Linguists have the job of learning all the different dialects so communications between clans go smoothly.

Uncle Tommy fought in World War II, was captured somewhere in Europe, and put in a prisoner of war camp. According to Lorraine, he stayed in the camp for a while, learned all the languages of the other prisoners, and then he was ready to leave. So he just left.

He escaped somehow and made his way back to Australia, where his nieces and nephews loved going to ethnic restaurants with him (and the restaurateurs loved it when he came), because he could speak to everyone in their own language.

She had other stories about her father, who was an initiated man in his own clan, as well as being a Methodist minister. When her father was ordained, his wife and children were not invited to attend the ceremony. He was a light-skinned man, which made him more acceptable to white authorities, while his wife, Lorraine's mother, was very dark-skinned and illiterate. Lorraine thinks this went against him, and might have been the reason he was never allowed to be the pastor of his own church.

Her father became a Methodist missionary, spreading the gospel to the Aborigines as he traveled from mission to mission. He taught only from the Book of Revelation, because it was the book in the Bible most like the traditional teachings of the Aborigines.

Lorraine's mother often led the Bible study classes. In the evenings before the classes, she would learn the relevant passages from the Bible by having her husband read them to her. During class the next day, she would sit with the Bible open on her lap as if she were reading, and quote verbatim what she had memorized the night before.

HUMPIES

YOU WOULDN'T BELIEVE IT.

I never lived in a house until I was six years old. We were living in these little humpies.

My Mum and Dad, they never had a house. No Aboriginal person had a house. A humpy is similar to a sweat lodge, made of sticks and wood—little round humpies.

On the mission, my dad was a little more well-off than others, because my dad was a Methodist minister. My parents went from mission to mission and opened up the church groups. When I was a kid, we traveled around in a big covered wagon, pulled by two horses. And sometimes we lived in tents.

Sometimes, Mum and Dad would make a little humpy,

and if they had to stay on a mission for three or four months or something, well, my Mum and the other women would go over to the town dump and get tins and bags and things like that and make a little house with them. A shack.

And when Mum and Dad were in a place called Armidale, right up in the New England country (an area just inland from the coast in Northern New South Wales), Dad was given a house to rent to start his missionary work. That was the first time we had been in a house. That house was spotless and we weren't allowed to even shuffle our feet in that house. My mum, she was very fussy.

CHURCH STORIES

WE WERE TOLD A LONG TIME AGO, OUR PEOPLE, THAT WE COULD LISTEN TO WHAT THE MISSIONARIES TEACH AND PREACH, GO TO CHURCH AND JOIN IN THE SONGS AND ALL THAT, BUT DON'T ACCEPT THE DOCTRINE, BECAUSE WE HAVE OUR OWN SPIRITUAL AND CULTURAL BELIEFS.

And that makes a lot of sense to me. It is only official when you have to sign papers or things like that, like when I applied for my passport. I had to put down a religion, so I put down

Church of England. We have to do that for our immigration department in case we drop dead somewhere, and they will call on a Church of England minister to say the last rites, I suppose. It won't matter to me. I will be dead.

I have been in a Catholic church a couple of times. Some of the mission managers were Catholics. If there weren't a church on the mission, they would take us to their Catholic church. There was one of the ones who wore a long brown suit, one of the Jesuits, I think. He used to come out and pick up some of the people and take them in to Church.

I remember that I went once. My head was full of what the old people said, "Don't accept the doctrine." And here was this priest in the Catholic Church swinging that little can with smoke in it, the incense, praying in the name of the Trinity, in the name of Father, the Son and the Holy Ghost. Well, that is a Spirit!

And yet the missionaries were saying to our old people, and to us younger ones, even, "Don't practice your spiritual beliefs, that's heathen, that belongs to the demons, the devil."

I was only a kid, but I couldn't sink that in, somehow. And with all the nuns standing in back with their black things on, what they were doing seemed a little like devil worship to me. I wrote something about that in my poem, "Might Be, Might Be, I Don't Know:"

Might Be, Might Be, I Don't Know

The preacher said that when I die
through pearly gates my soul would fly
and walk the streets of purest gold
where crystal waters flow.

Might be, might be, I don't know.

And in the Bible Book I look,
everywhere black devils fly
to heaven? Well...

Might be, might be, I don't know.

At one of these missionary churches, they would put all of the little kids, the three- to six-year-olds, in the front row.

In the next row would be next age group, up to ten or eleven, and then in the next row would be the teenagers. I was one of the little ones in the front row.

And there was a new Jesuit priest, who wore the brown robe and the round hat. He had a big red beard and his hair was baldy. He had that little round place. And he had a really big Scottish accent, and he would preach to all us kids like we were grownups. He would bang the Bible and we would all JUMP!

He would look straight at us and he would say, "Unless your sins are white as snow, you will never get to heaven."

But the way that he said that, it sounded like "Unless your *skins* are white as snow, you will never get to heaven."

He really scared the daylights out of us. Well, all us kids, we would run down to the creek and scrub and scrub, and some of the kids would run home and get flour to put on themselves. We were really frightened.

One of my aunts—she wasn't really my aunt, but I called her aunt, out of respect—she was reared up by the missionaries. There was an old organ in a corner of a room, and the missionaries taught her how to play. But they only taught her one song, how to play one hymn on that old organ, and that was "Onward, Christian Soldiers." Well, she would play the organ to "Onward Christian Soldiers, and we would all be singing "Jesus Loves Me" or "Where the Pearly Waters Flow." That was funny. We didn't think anything about it, you know, we were happily singing along whatever song we were singing and she would be playing "Onward Christian Soldiers." When I think back now, I crack up, but when I was a kid, it was nothing.

As long as Lorraine was willing to keep going, I was happy to be an attentive audience, until eventually we ran out of everything—tea, energy, even the inclination to smoke.

I drove her home and wished her well on her journey tomorrow. She wished me well on mine.

WEDNESDAY

I AM NOT REALLY SURE WHY I DECIDED TO REPEAT THE SAME trip that we had made the day before. I revisited Nimbin and stopped at Nimbin Rocks, where I hardly recognized the faces and shapes of the Old Man and Nimbunji. With Lorraine, they had been alive. Without her, they were just interesting rock formations.

A mountain turkey moved reluctantly out of the way as I pulled into the parking lot on Wollumbin. Although I had intended to spend the day breathing in sunshine from the top of mountain, I couldn't bring myself to make the climb. Twenty minutes into the forest, I turned around and came back out again, drove down the road a little ways and turned in at the *Sri Sathya Sai* sign.

The driveway went along the creek bank to a new two-story building in a large clearing in the woods. There was a garden and beds of flowers and a house with a big front porch further up the slope. A young woman in a print dress waved at me as she walked in a door of the nearer building.

I followed her in, was handed pamphlets, and was invited to look around. She apologized for the mess. In two days' time they were having a reception to inaugurate the first Sai School in Australia.

There were several people inside, busy at getting the room ready —a nice, simple, open room, with features well-crafted in wood and a lot of windows. A cheerful thirty-something man named Robert pointed out a painting of Sai Baba, the world teacher from India, and next to that a painting of Jesus Christ. He pointed to images representing six major religions of the world. Like pollen on the wind, their essence had found the way to the slopes of Wollumbin.

Robert was remarking that the teachings of Sai Baba honor "all faiths, races, creeds and all saints, sages, great men and women." I looked around and wondered if the Sai community would be interested in an opportunity to meet an elder from the Bundjalung clan.

Robert was curious about how I had turned up on their doorstep after only one month in Australia. I told him about coming to the area to find Lorraine. He hadn't heard of her. How had I?

"Actually, I think she is quite famous. She's been to the U.S. and Europe a number of times, teaching workshops," I answered.

"Naturally," he said, "it would be the Australians who wouldn't know anything about her."

It was Robert's mother who lived in the house behind the center. As I remember it, the story goes that she went to India to see Sai Baba, who told her that a Sai center was needed in Australia. Her response was, "How can I do that? I am just a little old lady," and Sai

Baba had stroked her head, saying, "Everything is all right."

Back in Australia, Robert's mother started having devotionals in her home. On another trip to India, $10,000 worth of items were stolen from her house, and she used the insurance money to begin building the center.

That was in 1988, and now they were starting the first Sai School in Australia. The center's devotional space would double as the schoolroom during the week. In two days' time, people from all over Australia, from as far as Perth three thousand miles away, would come for the school's inaugural reception.

As there were more people arriving to help with the preparations, I decided to give them a hand by getting out of their way. I thanked everybody and left, stopping at a cafe in nearby Uki to read through the Sai pamphlets over a cup of tea.

On page one of a pamphlet about the new school, the Mayor of Murwillumbah was mentioned. He was the politician that Lorraine and Elaine had discussed contacting about the cultural center, and he was to officiate the opening of the school on Friday. Page four of the pamphlet highlighted the importance of a relationship between the school and the natural environment surrounding the center.

What better person for the school to be acquainted with than the traditional custodian for Wollumbin? Lorraine knew its sacred stories and ceremonies. She also knew the plants that grew there and their traditional uses for healing.

A loose sheet entitled "Civic Responsibility" fell out of the pile of pamphlets, recommending service on a regular basis within the immediate community. There was a list of suggestions: humanitarian projects, tree plantings, child and animal sponsorship, and so on. I excavated a pen from my handbag and made my own addition to the bottom of the list — reconnecting children (all colors) to the land, through the ancient native traditions.

I finished my tea, and I had a plan. If the Sai group would have us and she wanted to come, I would bring Lorraine to the reception on Friday.

ALTHOUGH IT WAS ALREADY DARK WHEN I ARRIVED BACK AT THE MOTEL, I wanted to walk along the shore for a few minutes and feel the tide sucking the sand from under my feet. The footpath I followed to the beach lay ghostly and still under the scrub trees before opening out to a hard whistling wind blowing from the east over the sea.

There were clouds, rushing, hiding the stars. A few days before, the wooden steps at the end of the dunes had led me down to a wide smooth beach and contented little waves. Tonight the elements of wind and water were raw. The ocean pounded the beach and roared, exploding upward in towering sprays, shaping the darkness.

I convinced myself that, in this weather, there would be no good place for me to walk anyway, and raced my heart back through the dunes to bed.

THURSDAY

THE NEXT MORNING, IT WAS RAINING HARD. I CURLED UP ON the daybed and laughed my way through a book by Jane Gardam about a woman who slowly goes crazy and then gets better again. I hadn't heard from Lorraine since the night before last, and wondered if my time with her was over.

Gradually the rain stopped. Late in the afternoon there was a knock on the door, and there she was.

She was sorry she hadn't been by earlier. Her son, Dean, had had a mild heart attack. It had scared her. She was still trying to reassure herself that he was all right. Since yesterday she had been at the hospital or taking care of her grandchildren.

With her family in such turmoil, maybe having a place to come and just tell stories for a while was a help to her. However she was finding time to be with me, I was grateful for it. And grateful to her family, too.

I made the tea and scrounged for snacks in the little kitchenette, while shouting conversation through the bedroom to the sun porch where Lorraine was sitting.

"Did you make your meeting the other day?...That's good... No, I didn't make it to the top of Wollumbin. Let's just say I couldn't embrace the steepness of the climb. But I found out about the *Sri Satya Sai* sign. It's a spiritual center, for followers of Sai Baba...I don't know much about him, either, but I saw his picture, Lorraine, and I thought you'd like the fact that he is a black man, with frizzy hair. He looks like he could be from anywhere...There is a booklet on the daybed for you to look at. It's about a school that they are starting. They are having a reception on Friday and the Mayor of Murwillumbah will be there. I was wondering, would you like to go?...Well, good, me, too. So if you come get the tea, I will go down to the office and use the phone. I want to call and make sure it is okay."

The woman who answered the phone at the Sai Center was not enthusiastic about my wanting to come to the reception. Nothing personal, just that they were expecting a lot of people and had limited space. After a muffled conversation with somebody nearby, she said, "Well, all right, but please don't bring anyone else."

"Well, actually, I was hoping to bring an elder from the Bundjalung Clan," I replied. "She's the traditional custodian for Mount Warning."

The voice on the line went from ho-hum to thrilled. They would love to have us. I went back to the room to tell Lorraine the news.

She didn't stay long tonight. She wanted to get back to her

family, but she did take some time to tell me about her workshops, and what I refer to as "spirit matters."

WORKSHOPS

IF AM ASKED TO GIVE A WORKSHOP TO A GROUP OF WOMEN, I WILL TELL THEM FIRST THE CULTURAL WAY, THE WAY THE OLD WOMEN TAUGHT THE YOUNGER WOMEN.

It might be about looking after your body. It might be about looking after the children. It might be about looking after your husband, but that is not a very popular subject right now. So teaching is like that.

And sometimes I will say to the women, "I will show you what a woman's responsibility is to the Earth," and then I will give a little demonstration. I will say the Moon energy comes down to our hair which is the antenna and then passes through our body, that energy, into the ground, and that is the female energy, the Moon energy, that keeps the crystal grid in balance. Then I say to them, "We cannot do this without the menfolk."

Most times, I prefer a mixed group of male and

female, so that they come into balance at the same time. But there are times, too, when I need to talk to just women or just men. And in actual fact, my teachings and my responsibility are to bring men into balance, not so much the women. I was rather surprised when the old women said, "Lorraine, you concentrate on the men."

Women are out of balance with the men folk at the moment. So when I am talking to them, I just gently slip little things in. One thing that makes them happy is the fact that Aboriginal women's business and ceremonies are much, much stronger than the men's. Our men acknowledge that, and they respect us for that. We are the backbone, and they acknowledge that. It is good we have that equal balance.

For Western women, it is a bit hard now, what with the Women's Liberation Movement, which started in 1971, I think, in Australia.

SPIRIT MATTERS

I WILL TALK A BIT MORE ABOUT THE DIFFERENT SPIRITS.

We have got three different spirits.

First of all, there are spiritual guides from the planets, from the heavens. I just call them "friends."

Then there are the spirits of the ones who are dead. Their spirits are out there in the spirit world, waiting to be either reincarnated or staying out there as guides to different people, as Aboriginal guides to them.

And the third spirit is our self, our inner Spirit, our soul, our inner self. And that spirit needs constant guidance. You know, because we can't make up our own mind and because it is our brain that's going to tell our spirit and our bodies what to do.

So we need the constant guidance and teachings from the spirits, out of the spirit world. We believe in the Three—the planet beings and then the spirit human beings and Spirit.

I will tell you about how our spirit system works. This is our belief, how we get spirit teachings. Now, all of our old people, when we were living out on the missions, in our communities, well, the old people would sing out to everybody that they all must be in bed by seven o'clock at ni ght, just gone dusk. Everybody, the children, the teenagers, the old people, the young people, everybody should be in bed by seven o'clock, because they explained to us that this is the time when the ancestor spirits, the spirits of our mother or our father or our grandparents or loved ones that have gone, come back to be with us, to comfort us, to teach us, to look after us. And those ancestor spirits, those relation spirits, they come between the hours of seven o'clock at night right to about eleven.

See, we don't believe in dreams in the Western way of believing in dreams, we call it "spirit journeys" or "spirit teachings." And at these times between seven and eleven o'clock at night, our ancestors just simply come, take our spirits. They could take us for journeys or for teachings, or they give us predictions or anything like that. They could take us into the future, they could take us right back into the past, and they could just keep us in the present. So we have to be prepared if we want the ancestor spirits to come to us and to teach us.

We have to be prepared. We have to be in bed, so they know where to find us. It is no good us sitting up in a bar, or dancing in a disco, or at the pictures, or anywhere out visiting, because our ancestor spirits are not going to run all around the city to look for us, and then we lose very valuable teachings. This modern world is confusing to them, to the ancestor spirits.

So those of us who wanted to, like me, I had to be in bed, it didn't matter what I wanted to be doing, I couldn't, because my teachings were strict. So I used to go to bed early, and sure enough they would come and they would take me all over the place.

They took me and showed me how Atlantis went down, they said that Atlantis was a very wicked city and it is not going to rise again like a lot of people think that it is. It is not. They showed me a lot of things, and those things have come to pass. I need not tell you what they were because you already know it.

Now, the spirit ancestor teachings, they stop around

eleven o'clock or nearer midnight, like that. That gives our bodies time to have a good rest, a peaceful sleep, because around about four o'clock in the morning, in between four o'clock and six o'clock in the morning, our planetary guides, our planetary beings, come down and teach.

See, they don't actually teach anything (that is up to the ancestor spirits), but what they do is program our minds like a computer, and then when they want us to do that specific job or give particular teachings, they just simply sort of snap their fingers and that reawakens the teachings that they put in our minds. And we automatically do the work that they want us to do. We think of it as thought patterns, thoughts coming from our minds.

Well, the people that are chosen to do that, like myself, when they come and program my mind, they talk into my mind. For the women, it is a man's voice telling us what to do. And for the men, it is a woman's voice telling them what to do. This is so we won't get mixed up with our own thinking and all the little chatty voices that go on in your head. And so, we are able to distinguish the voice of the planetary beings talking to us.

We might not remember immediately what they want us to do. They could leave it for about a week, two weeks, three weeks, six months, and then when the time is right, when they want us to use or put into practice the messages that they have given us, then they awaken our brains real quick, so we remember what they told us and we do it.

Well, that is the other form of teachings. And that is a good one, I think, and so do they, because that is how they have operated for thousands and thousands of years.

On the missions, we had our spiritual teachings, but in secret. The missionaries had their houses there and usually a church built there, but a lot of times when the missionaries would go home, that would be when our teachings would start.

And although we weren't allowed to go off the mission because there were government agents on the mission, we had nighttime. About eight other women and myself, we would go out into the bush and have the vision teachings and stay out there with the old women. So that is when they gave a lot of their teachings.

And then I was lucky. I went to make films and got jobs in big film productions, like with ABC (Australian Broadcasting Company), and I would go with the crew. That gave me the opportunity to meet all the other teachers, all around Australia, and they taught me. Only five minutes or ten minutes, a half an hour I would need to be with them, and they would teach me basics, and I would come back and I would tell Auntie Millie, who was my teacher. Then she would talk to the spirits, the spirits would talk to her, she would talk to me, and then I would carry the instructions out. That is how we worked it. It was good.

See, for the Aboriginal people, the women follow the mother's line, and they continue on the women's ceremony.

When I wanted to go out, well, then my husband would look after the kids, or my father-in-law, my sister-in-law, my sister. They were ready to take over the family straightaway, and I could go with Auntie Millie two or three weeks on end.

Now a lot of our old sites are lived on. People own the properties. Some of them are kind people and will let us do our ceremony, but most would say "No, you are trespassing, you can't go there."

Our elders could revive all that, the ceremonies at the old sites, the sacred sites. They could do that for white people as well as black people, because we are all going to be one people in the new world. We can't be separated, segregated.

FRIDAY

ELAINE DECIDED TO COME TO THE SAI SCHOOL RECEPTION with us and help Lorraine corral some good connections. While Lorraine sat waiting in a ring of vacated chairs, Elaine greeted, smiled, and steered people in Lorraine's direction.

The principal of the new school and a top administrator of the Sai Organization Australia wanted to know the traditional stories and about workshops and about children's books that Lorraine had written. The mayor of Murwillumbah was ready to get together and talk about a cultural center, any time.

Lorraine and Elaine were so efficient at getting things lined up, I was free to wander, to introduce myself and to shake hands with Frances Parry, the radiant woman who had started the Sai Center on Wollumbin.

Everyone I met asked the same question—how was it that I was there, after only one month in the country, especially in the company of the traditional custodian for the mountain? Nothing I answered sounded quite right, except that now Lorraine knew the Sai community and they knew her.

Even if the Aboriginal cultural center didn't work out, maybe there were other things that might.

SATURDAY

THIS MORNING, I WENT WITH LORRAINE TO A POLITICAL meeting at the Old Community Hall in Byron Bay. For the first half hour, I sat upright and attentive while twenty-five or thirty other people talked about Aboriginal Rights and land conservation. It was quickly apparent that these were topics that ignited the fire in everyone's nature.

There were a series of polite but heated discussions, on issues that require forgiveness and probably a lot of money to resolve. I went from feeling fine to having a blinding headache and had to leave to get a Coke.

Afterward, Lorraine said that her involvement in politics might be the cause of some of her health problems. Her Band kept telling her that she needed to stick to spiritual matters. Nevertheless, the subject of politics inspired her to tell me a good story as we drove to get Elaine.

AFTER LEAVING THE MISSIONS

IN 1971, WE HAD JUST COME OFF MISSIONS.

And on our missions we didn't have nice houses, just four walls and one room with no electricity, no water. No nothing. We would sleep in one corner.

We couldn't bathe much, because there was just one community tap and shower place in the middle of the mission. There was a big fireplace, for an open fire, and we all cooked there and washed up in a shed somewhere.

It was terrible. And we lived on rations that the government supplied — flour, tea, sugar, but no vegetables or anything else.

We lived like that. And we were only given our freedom in 1970, after the 1967 Referendum.

You can imagine — living in humpies with no electricity, nothing, then walking off a mission and into a house — our old people, especially the older people, they were totally lost. They didn't know how to count money and things like that.

Talk about a revelation, the early 1970s. They were good days though, days of learning. All through that confusion, our old people had the teachings from above, the spiritual teachings, to help all the younger people like myself through it. We were sorting out the different ones of us. Who were going to be teachers? Who were going to be leaders? It was good.

I was a Board Director of the Aboriginal Medical Service in Redfern (Aboriginal area in Sydney), and it was in 1971 that the Women's Liberation Group met in a town hall in Sydney. There must have been three or four hundred women of different sections. So I was asked to speak on the Medical Service, and all the women said, "Lorraine, you have got the biggest mouth, you go and talk."

So I got up in front of all these women, and I said, "Ladies, if you give us Aboriginal women decent homes, press-button appliances, our men jobs, and our children a decent education with three feeds in their stomach everyday, I will show you a liberated woman. You're looking at her."

I was speaking the truth. We were struggling. Our men couldn't get jobs. They were going on the dole, on welfare.

I came straight off a mission when my three boys were little and went to Sydney, where I got a job. We lived in a flat, and it had a gas stove. There is a paper called the *Sydney Morning Herald*, a really big thing, and I would roll the paper up and turn the gas on, burn a bit of the paper on the end and stand right the way back, looking away, while trying to light the stove with the end of the paper. I was so frightened of that gas stove.

In 1972, we were doing a course in Aboriginal Arts at the Black Theatre Arts & Crafts Center, which I helped start. We were coming really out in politics and we had a lot of street theatre about that. We used to have lawyers come to the Black Theatre and talk to the young people and tell us our legal rights. So things were getting really warm.

I don't know how it happened, but one day the Commonwealth Police walked straight into the theatre and said that the director of the Black Theatre, Betty Fisher, and I had been accused of letter-bombing a premier or senator from Queensland.

I burst out laughing. A picture of me standing straight back while trying to light my gas stove had come to my mind, and I thought, "How in the world do they think I have the knowledge to rig up a bomb? We are just getting used to switching a light on, using electricity."

We talked to them a bit and we all had a good laugh. So they left us alone.

WE WERE GOING NEXT TO A BIG WOMEN'S FAIR IN ONE OF THE LARGER towns inland from Byron Bay. Lorraine and Elaine continue to thank me for chauffeuring them, although I don't know how they tolerate the way I drive on the left side of the road. They never complain about the heart-stopping moments in traffic. I have noticed, however, that Lorraine always sits defensively, hand pushed against the dashboard or gripping the armrest on the door. It must be exhausting.

Elaine had organized a workshop about women for Lorraine to lead, along with several other Aboriginal elders, one with snowy white hair that I had seen at the meeting this morning. A dozen or so participants, all young and all white, some with children, gathered at the designated spot. We went together to a little city park, to sit on the ground in a henge of flat stones. The elders said they were sacred stones that had been moved there when the park had been created.

It was a fine day for being outside. Things were going smoothly. I was especially admiring Elaine's abilities as a facilitator when one of the young women said that she lived near Taylor Lakes and wanted to go there in a sacred and respectful way. She wanted to visit other female sites that way, too, and so did her friends. Could someone tell them how to do that?

Hey, I thought, this person could be another solution to something that Lorraine and I had been discussing all week. Just a few nights ago, Lorraine had talked about the elders reviving the ceremonies for the benefit of everyone. If, as she said, Aboriginal women weren't allowed to gather at sacred sites for ceremony, maybe a group of white women could. What if white women organized the events, and invited Lorraine and other elders as guests to lead the ritual? A Sacred Sites Group for this area. Wouldn't that work? Was anybody doing that around here?

For some reason I couldn't understand, no one answered the woman's question. Lorraine said later that it had something to do with protocol. After some moments, there was a vague acknowledgement from Lorraine that the question had been asked, and then the conversation moved elsewhere. Maybe another chance would come round to ask the question again.

THE WORKSHOP FINISHED EARLY ENOUGH FOR ME TO RETURN TO the beach in the Suffolk Park area for the afternoon. I wanted to make my own pilgrimage to the Taylor Lakes.

They are called tea tree lakes, because freshwater streams wash oil from the nearby forests of tea trees into the lake basins. Aboriginal women once went there for healing and to give birth. Men were only allowed to enter the lakes before going into battle, to purify their intentions, and right after, to wash away the taint of death before returning to their families.

Lorraine had told me that the lakes were on private land, although one of them at least was easy to reach from the public beach at Broken Head. I just followed a broad wash through the dunes and walked straight into the tangy, astringent water, which was as clear and richly brown in color as a cup of good tea.

Completely surrounded by the tea trees, the lake was wide and round, shallow in some spots, over my head in others. There was no one else around. Under a cloudless blue sky I floated for a while, as still as I could get, feeling the oil find the places on my body that needed healing.

THE OTHER LAKE WAS AT THE END OF A LONG, DEEP CHANNEL OF water that was choked with weeds and roots that caught at my feet and rubbed against my legs. I swam shrieking and shuddering with every kick.

The second lake was much smaller than the first. It felt cut off and isolated, hemmed in by the brushy, thick tea tree forest that crowded its banks. This lake was where the three murdered Aboriginal women had been thrown.

Once I got there I didn't particularly want to stay, and the pair of sea eagles flew by, pointing me south again, to the other lake. Before I went, I decided to be there as a member of the Sacred Sites Group and ask for a healing and blessing of this sacred place. I said a prayer, and energy, like steam rising, released from the surface of the lake.

Things felt better after that. I didn't mind so much the hidden places among the roots as I swam back along the channel to the big lake and the beach.

SUNDAY

LORRAINE WANTED TO SPEND THE WHOLE DAY TAKING ME TO sacred sites in Bundjalung country, the ones I hadn't seen yet. She came knocking on my door bright and early, wearing the frog T-shirt I had given her, so big it came almost to her knees and hid the nubby knit pink shorts she was wearing underneath. She said the outfit made her feel risqué, a risqué grandma. I took a picture of her in it, sitting in the armchair.

I can't remember the name of the little town we went to first, one of the quiet untouristed ones, like Suffolk Park, that line the coast south of Byron Bay. We were there to see the women's Bora Ring.

Mudrooroo describes Bora Rings as "the sacred ceremonial grounds of the Australian Aborigine." This one was surrounded by a chain link fence and located between two small houses on a residential street. Once inside the fence, an area no more than fifteen feet wide and sixty feet long, the swing sets and deck chairs in the yards on either side seemed very far away.

A light, sweet wind was blowing. A path meandered under the cool shade of a few trees to the Bora Ring, a simple circle of slightly mounded earth only a few inches high and a few feet across, forming an O about ten feet wide.

I took off my shoes and walked around the top of the mound as Lorraine told me I could, feeling the tenderness of the lush green grass. It was so peaceful there, an oasis of peace in the middle of a subdivision.

Our next stop was a men's Bora Ring, across the coastal highway and inland towards Lismore. Getting there was nice. The day was warm and bright with my favorite kind of big blue summer sky, filled with rows of fluffy little cottonball clouds. There wasn't much traffic. The road went straight, way up, then way down, up and down with the land. At the top of a rise, Lorraine said to turn at the graveyard, onto a short gravel drive that stopped at the edge of the Men's Bora Ring.

The men's site was two or three times larger than the women's, covered with grass that bent over and rippled like wind on water. On the far side of the ring was a semicircle of slender eucalyptus trees, the kind koalas like, and beyond that, the crest of the hill and a wide green valley of open fields and dark stands of trees, falling gently away for miles in every direction.

Men's Bora Ring

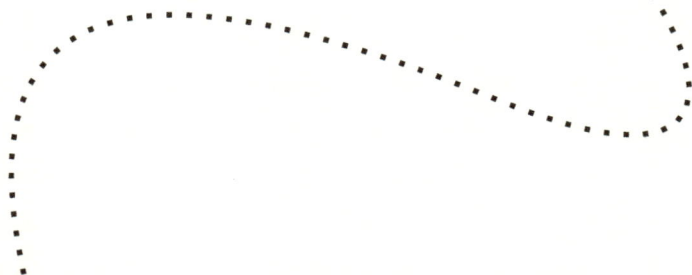

There is only a slight groove here, just a slight one, around the outside, where the men used to walk around.

In the middle, if you can see that little dark hollow there, that is where the fire was.

This is not a ring for sacred ceremony, but a place where the men and boys came together. On the headland out there, the men of the host tribes would sit there to welcome in the young men, the young men who came from every part of Australia down to here. The older men who sat out there could see right across that valley and to those far mountains way over there. They could see the campfires at night, and even in the day, they could see the smoke going up, and those signs would tell them that the young men were traveling. The older men would sit down and make a fire and that would be the sign to let the young men and boys know where to come.

So when they all got together and everybody was here and accounted for, well, young men and boys would come into the ring through that little opening in the Bora Ring and introduce themselves in their own dance. They used to dance their stories and their lineage here on this place.

The singer would sing things like, "We are from the Northern Territory," or "We are from the Kimberly Country and this is our totem," and they would dance that.

And then when they had a couple of days of introduction here and they were all accounted for, the older men would take them and they would go straight across country that way, across the Richmond Valley to the initiation ground at Nimbin. There they would get their higher teachings or the teachings that they came all the way down to the East Coast for.

NEITHER ONE OF US STEPPED ONTO THE MOUNDED EARTH OF THE men's Bora Ring or even went inside where the fire had been kept. We walked around the perimeter, in the shade of the perfect crescent of well-spaced eucalyptus trees, looking for signs of the family of koalas that had once lived there. The trees appeared young — smooth bark, lively branches, no gaps in the semi-circle to suggest a dying and a rotting away. Lorraine says, however, that they are magical and have been there since ancient times without aging.

We took a break, sitting on the side of the hill looking out, imagining campfire smoke arising in the distance.

"Can you believe they, the white people, I mean, put a graveyard up here?" Lorraine asked me.

I could. It was a beautiful place, peaceful, as the women's ring had been.

"A lot of white people might think you can only have this kind of peace when you are dead," I answered.

Our last stop was to be the Goanna Headland, in the Bundjalung National Park. Just a few months ago, when my trip had drawn its first breaths and emerged Goanna-shaped from the big Australian map on my wall, Adelaide had been the tip of its tail and the Goanna Headland had been its nose. Now we were going there, back along the roly-poly road to the coast.

First we stopped at a lookout, built of concrete and metal railings, just to the north of the Headland.

THE GOANNA HEADLAND

HERE WE ARE AT GOANNA HEADLAND, WHICH IS ALSO EVANS HEADLAND.

A long, long, long time ago, there was the Goanna. She was female. She was a Bundjalung woman. Her husband was from the hill country, way up in the hills. And he was the male Goanna.

Well, the story goes that the husband and wife had a big fight, and the female came down here to her own country, where her people were. She came down here as a woman, running all the way from up in the hills. When she got here, she found that all her family was away. The men were out hunting and the women were out doing some fishing, out there in the ocean in canoes. The woman, the female Goanna, got very hurt because she couldn't reach her family. So she just sort of laid down on the beach and died.

When she died, her body became the headland that you see there. If you look closely you will see her back with the head going down and her nose, and the little parts of green there on the side, those are her little hands, the little Goanna hands.

This is what we call the Goanna Headland. This is the female Goanna, but that doesn't mean to say that this is a woman's place. It's not. It is for everybody.

And the story goes, too, that the husband, the male Goanna, didn't chase the woman down to the sea, but stayed up in his own country. When he died, he went into a big mountain called Goanna Mountain, up there where Auntie Millie comes from. Because he is Auntie Millie's ancestor and she talked to that mountain, the golden Goanna would come out and show itself on a rock. I have seen it many a time.

This husband and wife, when they died in human form, they both turned back into Goanna. She is here and he is up there in the hills, which is one of the regions of our people.

The Goanna Headland is a nice place. We would like to keep it as it is, especially because this is where the dolphins' cave is, on the side of the headland there, near the Goanna's nose. This is the cave where Mary Wilson, who was dolphin custodian, used to come.

Well, Mary was the last woman to do that. There are probably others in other parts of Australia, other keepers, but I don't know where they are. She was the one for the East Coast, anyway. These places are handed down to different people's care over the years, but it must only be through the lineage.

She told me that inside this cave, it opens up and there is a big lake, and that this is where the mother dolphins used to come to have their babies. And when there were no dolphins there, mums having their babies, a lot of sharks and whales used to go into this cave as well, for safety, especially during the time that the whales were being hunted for their blubber. Then they could come back out whenever they wanted to and go back out to the deep sea.

So every so often, Mary Wilson would come down from inland to the coast and stay in this cave so she could talk with the dolphins and hear their messages and the prophecies and learn what was going on in the world, all that sort of stuff. And she was told here, oh, it must be about a year before the Harmonic Convergence (1987), that the sacred sites and the energy grids and all that would be activated with the help of human beings, and the dolphins would then take that energy through the water and hit solid ground on other continents. The energy from the people involved with the Harmonic Convergence would spread all throughout the world to activate all the spots on the energy grids and the ley lines, that system.

The Earth now has been getting help from human beings since that time, and it is rectifying itself. It is going through its change of life and getting ready to create a new world.

So the Earth is rejuvenating and it is up to us now, us Medicine People and the people that are working for that sort of cause, to get humanity into balance.

WHEN I LOOKED THROUGH THE WRONG END OF THE TELESCOPE ALL those years ago, I had seen Australia. I had changed my name to Goanna and traveled thousands of miles to find a woman in whom I saw myself.

And here she was, telling me a story that I recognized, the story of all the times I had turned away in pain, instead of saying how I felt, and died to any resolution because of it. A traditional Bundjalung story was matching up the pieces of my own wounded heart.

All week long, Lorraine had been talking about the need for balance, and for healing between the male and the female, but the female Goanna goes away and the male Goanna doesn't come looking. They die, forever apart.

Still true to the old ways (mine), I didn't want to talk about it. Instead, I told Lorraine about my vision, about the dolphins and the tiny woman on the beach with the glowing coal of a stone in her palm.

"Was that Mary Wilson?" I asked.

"Yes, yes, that's her," Lorraine told me. "The stone is a piece of the rosy quartz, from the heart of Wollumbin. She often appears to people that way."

"Why do you think that she came to me?" I asked her. "All she said was to feed the dolphins."

"I don't know, really," she answered, then added, "I guess you will have to figure that out for yourself."

And then she told me another story.

DOLPHINS

A STORY ABOUT GOANNA HEADLAND GOES THAT A LONG, LONG, LONG, LONG TIME AGO, THERE WAS A TRIBE THAT CAME FROM THE INLAND OF AUSTRALIA, IN NEW SOUTH WALES.

One year, they came down to the beach in the summer to stay while it was cold up in their country, to have a holiday on the beach here. This time, with this tribe from inland, two brothers came.

See, the Bundjalung people were the host, and they used to let the other tribes camp all around the place. And it was the custom, early in the morning, for the little children to get up and all go down to the beach and sing a song to the dolphins. They would pat the water, beat their hands on the water like playing a drum, and the little children would sing this song. Well, the women and the men, anybody, would hold their nets and before long, they would see the dolphins bringing in all the fish for them to eat.

Those two brothers from inland, they were totally fascinated by the dolphins driving the fish in for the people to eat. They thought there was a human being inside, a human spirit inside these dolphins. So one day, they got up real early in the morning and they sang a song to the dolphins, and a dolphin came in. And these two brothers, they speared the dolphin and took it in to a cave, not the one here, but another one up the beach a bit, between Lennox Head and Broken Head. So they took it up there to the little cave and they cut it open. And they were really shocked to see that it was just a big fish.

So they knew the damage that they had done, and they were frightened and ran away back home to their own country. Their mother was there in the camp near the beach, but nobody was the wiser about those two boys.

Early next morning, all the children got up and down to the beach they went, arguing about whose turn it was to sing. So some little fellow, it was his turn, one of the little Bundjalung boys. He was singing and singing and nothing happened. Then all the little children were singing and clapping the water and nothing happened. The old men were sitting up on the bank watching, and the other people were sitting there watching, and nothing happened.

And so the children went home, and two of the old men walked up the beach a bit and they sang a song and called in the dolphins. And one old man dolphin, he came in and he said, "Look, one of our people has been speared by two young men from your camp, and we will never bring in any more fish for you to eat."

Well, they were all upset when the two old men came back to the camp and told everyone what had happened. And this old woman, she started crying and she started wailing. The old men went up to her and said, "Sister, what is wrong with you?"

She said, "The ones that killed that dolphin, they are my two sons. They are not here. That is how I know that it is them. They are gone."

One of the old men, one of the elders, said, "Well, sister, you know what we have got to do."

And she said, "Yes, I know that you have to kill those boys. They broke the law and they have to be punished."

So the old men called out four young warriors and told them what happened, and they said to the young warriors, "You go and hunt those boys, and when you see them, you kill them."

So, the four young men went. Three days they were gone. And for three days the old woman sat beside a fire and she was crying and crying.

The young warriors found those two young boys, and they killed them. They brought back the spear that had killed the dolphin and showed it to the old woman, and she said, "Yes, that is my sons' spear. And they are the ones responsible for the death of the dolphin and the hunger of the people."

The old men said, "Now sister, you have to go and tell the dolphins that the boys are dead and it is finished."

So the old woman went down to the beach, and she was singing and crying and singing and crying, and the old dolphins, they were stubborn and they wouldn't come and see her. They wouldn't, for a long time. And she came down to the beach three or four times, and just before sundown at the end of this day, well, two old dolphins came in.

The old woman said, "I am sorry about my boys. They are dead now, so can you forgive us? Every year I will come back here, and I will cry and wail the mourning, wailing song, and I will cry for my dead sons, and I will cry for the dead dolphin. And that will be my way of showing respect."

So that was all right. The dolphins said, "We will forgive you. We will come here, but we won't bring fish anymore."

So everybody made their peace with the dolphins, and the dolphins made their peace with the people. Incidentally, our people never called them dolphins. They called them porpoises. So anyway, every year, every summertime, the old lady would come down and she would go and sing the song, the forgiveness song, to the dolphins.

When she died, it was passed on to her daughter, and she would come down and sing the forgiveness song and then her granddaughter. Down, down, down the female line until there were no more women of that line left. So the responsibility came back to the Bundjalung women.

Then the Bundjalung women used to come down and sing that song for that old lady and for her tribe, until it came right down to the present time today. The last one to sing that song was Mary Wilson, and Mary is dead now, Sister Mary who died in 1991.

She wanted to hand that responsibility on to me, but I had a lot of responsibilities of my own, a lot of teachings to do and a lot of places I had to be. I wouldn't have been able to do a good job. So Sister Mary said, "Maybe it is best to let go, let it go. Maybe it is best not to pass it on to anybody."

And I think it is the best thing. The country has changed, and we have changed, big changes. The stories aren't dead, but that part of the responsibilities, the custodianship, must go now.

Anyway, that is the story of the dolphins.

As much as I wanted to, there could be no turning away and dying to the truth in this story, this time. Lorraine's dolphin story felt like my dolphin story turned inside out.

In the place of miracles and Mr. and Mrs. Love, there was distrust and disrespect, followed by retribution and years of singing the forgiveness of an ancient wrong. This story was meant to frighten, like the gun in my own tale.

"A story meant to disorient and disarm," I thought to myself, and laughed at the paradox.

In the Bundjalung story, the dolphins had fed the people. Mary Wilson had told me to feed them, while holding a stone that represented the balance between the male and the female.

I wanted to understand. I knew Lorraine would tell me again that I would have to figure it out for myself.

"Mary let it go, the custodianship for the dolphins?" I asked.

"Yes, she let it go," Lorraine replied.

WE LEFT THE LOOKOUT, DRIVING DOWN AND AROUND THROUGH THE open heathlands of the park, to a beach of smooth stones and a cove of sand. Across the stones was the Headland. Lorraine was tired, and it was raining a little. She said, "Why don't you go see what you can see and I will wait here."

So I set off across the sand and the stones, stepping up and out onto the boulder-sized rocks around the Headland's base, hoping to get beyond its point and catch a glimpse of the dolphins' cave.

First I scrambled in one direction, then, looking for the easiest way, backed up to try another. The tide was coming in, crashing against the rocks and making them slippery, revealing them, and covering them up again.

I went as far as I could, taking a long time to get there, and then stood wondering if that shadowed crevice on the sheer face of the Headland was the mouth of the cave. Maybe it wasn't.

When I turned around to return to the beach, I saw another way to get back there, one I hadn't noticed before. It lay closer into the curve of the Headland, where the water was quiet and the rocks were dry and lined up like stepping stones for a path through a garden.

Well, there you go. Hindsight is like that.

I returned by the gentler route.

Monday

"Lorraine, I think I'll return the car tomorrow and take the train to Sydney. It's been a wonderful week, an incredible week."

"It's time for you to go, then?"

"Feels like it."

"I think that I've shown you a pretty good time. I think that I've done a good job with that."

"You've shown me everything and included me in everything. How could I ever find the words to thank you enough?"

"So now you have the stories. You have my permission to use them, whatever way you want to."

"Lorraine? Thank you again, for everything."

AT THE END

MARCH 18, 1997

M Y PLAN WAS TO SPEND TWO, MAYBE THREE DAYS IN Sydney. I didn't think I would want to stay in a big city for very long. On the train down, I imagined myself looping in and out of the Circular Quay at atomic speeds, trying to visit as many places as possible in the shortest amount of time.

I would say hello to Biannca Pace and go to the library to see Aunt Millie deliver her line about Elvis in the film *Eelemarni*. Then I would rent a car and take the scenic coastal highway south, maybe stopping at Wilson's Promontory, on the coast of Victoria. Like Wilpena Pound, it has something to do with Sirius and Lemurian knowledge, and I still felt pulled by that.

After a day or so in Melbourne, a train would take me back to Adelaide to say goodbye to Karen and Peter before I flew home.

Sydney, however, is going to be my last stop. I hadn't counted on loving it here. It's beautiful—a city whose center is water.

I am staying at the Cremorne Point Manor, right across the harbor from the Sydney Opera House on the North Shore, where Lorraine wants to live. As it turns out, the quick and easy way for me to go anywhere in the city is to walk three minutes to the end of the point and get on a ferry. Riding the ferries is so much fun that sometimes I will take one to Circular Quay and back just to see the flocks of sailboats skimming across the water or to watch the sun set behind the Sydney Harbor Bridge. I know I am not the only one.

Another reason I have stayed is that I have found the stone, the one I dreamed about on the way to Alice Springs. The one I used to cut the spirit cord.

It was right there in Biannca's store, in a glass case with a spotlight on it directly across from the front door.[5] I was able to hold it for a while, and it sat in my palm feeling just as I had remembered it from the dream—like the handle of a utility knife.

Biannca handed me a book by Katrina Raphael that described it as dogtooth calcite, or stellar beam calcite, useful in "…finalizing the completion of the old and renewing life in their sharply defined terminations that point to a new beginning…and shaping an undeniable new reality, whose essence, statement and purpose, is of unified spirit and matter."

After awhile, I thought to ask where it had come from, and Biannca said, "Elmwood, Tennessee."

"Elmwood, TENNESSEE?" I said, my voice high and squeaky with amazement.

"Tennessee," she repeated. "It came from a zinc mine there,

sometime during the 1950s."

When I heard that, that the stone had come from the Earth a little less than an hour from where I live, I knew my journey was over.

I had followed my Goanna songline from tip to nose, gathering up fragments of myself, wounds and strengths, and now the stone was promising me a new reality and a new beginning. The old way, the old song, had served its purpose. If Mary Wilson could let it all go, then I could.

Maybe what I had come this far to learn was that I could feed the dolphins — and feed me, too — by bringing the male and the female, the above and below, back into balance with each other. By opening up, instead of always experiencing the separation.

I was ready to shake myself free of a Goanna's life, and take an awakening sense of wholeness back home to Tennessee.

IN THE MEANTIME, I AM CONTENT TO DRINK TEA AND READ JANE Gardam books at the cafe in the Royal Botanical Gardens. Or meander the walking trail that follows the coastline of the North Shore, in around the coves and out along the points of land that separate them, as if tracing the fingers of a giant's hand. That's how I found Little Sirius Cove, a few peninsulas over from Cremorne Point, where the *Sirius,* the flagship for Captain James Cook's exploring fleet, first landed.

Above the cove is Little Sirius Point, a wild sliver of land with a good view of the city in the distance across the harbor. On the other side of the cove, high up and secluded, a large rock the shape of a dolphin leaps out from the hillside.

At the end of a journey that has lasted thirty-four years, I am happy to sit for a while in the grass near the dolphin-shaped rock and remember the grass on the mounded earth of the Women's Bora Ring, as soft as the circle in the center of a mother's kiss.

MARCH 20, 1997

SAVED THE LITTLE PILE OF HOWARD MURPHET'S BOOKS I'D
bought in Sydney for the plane ride home, so I was several
miles above the Pacific Ocean when I read the stories of Sai
Baba arriving on a motorcycle to offer a helping hand; and another
one about the bewildered man who thought he was traveling for
business and found himself delivering a package from Sai Baba to a
total stranger instead.

Memories of my trip suddenly lined themselves up like the
stepping stones through a garden—the Harley-Davidson T-shirt in
my meditation; the mystery man on the motorcycle buying a motel
across from the Sai center on Wollumbin; the link between the same
motel and Lorraine, the mountain's traditional custodian; me, who
was headed in that direction anyway, ready to rent a car and visit
Wollumbin and on the lookout for anything to do with Sai Baba.

To be honest, I don't know how I feel about it, this hindsight or insight, whatever it is. After the initial rush of an oh-this-is-cool sense of clarity, sheepishness, in the fullest meaning of that word, has settled in.

MAY 7, 1997

I CAME HOME TO MARRIAGES. THE FIRST, MY NIECE'S, AND TODAY, my sister's. Here is my gift to share with them, written with love, from Anne.

THIS MARRIAGE

May this marriage be one
that you can put your elbows on
and fill yourselves
with the simple things in life.

A marriage under which
you can kick off your shoes
and feel with your toes
the life you are creating together.

A marriage that you can dance
and sing around
and hold hands

and pray around
and give thanks. A marriage
around which you can invite your friends
and share with them the bounty,
so that they can give thanks too.

May this marriage stand foursquare and sturdy
amidst the little murders of the mind
and the bigger battles of the heart. Stand
in the morning sun to warm you
and reflect the peace of coming together.

In strength
and breadth
may this marriage serve you
and serve to you a Feast—
                    Faith,
                     Honor,
                      Courage,
                       Truth,
                        Joy,
              Love abide.

BEYOND

MARCH 15, 2000

THE TRIP TO AUSTRALIA HAS BECOME A BOOK, AND ONCE again, I want to get in touch with Lorraine. It's important to me that she feels respected by what I have written.

The dilemma (I think) might be in finding her again. This time, however, after one email to Biannca Pace, I have her new telephone number and address and am talking to Lorraine the next morning. If reaching her had been this easy three years ago, I might not have had much to write about. So I thank her for being hard to find in the beginning and now for being so accessible.

We have the funniest conversation. Although Lorraine recalls my name, she doesn't remember much else about me or about the time that we spent together. I laugh and laugh about that, in light of my having thought about her and her family and Australia just about every day during the last few years because of this writing project. I comment that she might enjoy the book more because she has forgotten what we did, and then we both laugh. It is fun talking to her again.

Since last seeing Lorraine, she has applied to reclaim thirty acres of land and the Taylor Lakes from the Crown, with the intention of returning them to their traditional purpose, as Women's Land. I wish her well, envisioning the lakes being honored once again in a sacred and respectful way.

By the end of the conversation, Lorraine remembers me. "Oh, yes," she says. "You were a woman on a very deep journey."

FEBRUARY 2001

L AST SATURDAY NIGHT, FOR THE FIRST TIME IN A VERY LONG while, I had a dream about Lorraine.

In the dream Lorraine is traveling with two other Aboriginal women, and they are all here in Nashville for a visit. Lorraine is content to stay in my guest room, while her two traveling companions prefer to make camp in my back yard. There is a cooking fire and tents, and I wonder briefly what the neighbors will think.

One of the women is tall and quite young looking, and the other is small and appears very ancient. Could it be Mary Wilson? Maybe even Aunt Millie?

The ultimate reason Lorraine has come here to Tennessee is, of course, to realize Auntie Millie's dream to visit Graceland. And I am the one with the car. So we all pack up and head toward Memphis, stopping on the way for a brief, casual visit with Al and Tipper Gore.

Awake on Sunday morning, I feel particularly happy about the meeting with the Gores. After all, Al Gore and Lorraine share a similar dream of an Earth in Balance. And curiously, on my return from Australia, I had learned that Elmwood, Tennessee, the origin of the spirit-cord-cutting stone, is the Gores' home community.

TODAY, TUESDAY, I RECEIVE AN EMAIL FROM BIANNCA PACE IN Australia telling me Lorraine died peacefully last Thursday in a hospital in Byron Bay.

The shock at the news feels like a physical blow. She is too young! Maybe sixty or so?

I wonder at the timing of her passing just as the first edition of the book, *Unconventional Means*, is finding its way out into the world. Lorraine had said that she liked what I had written—in her words, a truthful book, a woman's book about women.

Although I am very, very sad, after a few hours I begin to feel glad, too.

In my dream, Lorraine has been able to make the trip to Graceland for her beloved Aunt Millie, and she has spent a few minutes with an influential American politician whose interests match her own. The stories that she entrusted to me have been shared.

Enriched, as always, by Lorraine's ever-lively presence, I wish her much joy on her journey. I am ever thankful that she has been part of mine.

NOTES

GETTING THERE

1. Radnor Lake Natural Area, Nashville, Tennessee.

2. Chris Faulconer is an ordained minister, a gifted healer, counselor, ceremonialist, dynamic teacher and group leader. She has developed a healing process, "Journeying," which combines ancient shamanic wisdom and personal empowerment. Chris developed the curriculum for the Rev. Rosalyn Bruyere's Crucible Program, and lectured for the program for fourteen years.

3. Suzee (aka Suchi) Waters Benjamin is a multi-talented artist who has been using the creative process for the past twenty years to create a bridge from spirit to form as a means of healing,

transforming, and building community. As a singer, songwriter, multimedia visual artist, healer and teacher, she believes in the power of the healing arts and creative arts to tap the source of beauty within, so that co-creating with the divine can be experienced. Suchi's healing practice focuses on the "sacred path of the heart...the path made visible through the art of living."

THERE

TUESDAY: WOLLUMBIN

4. The word "Nrrahpul" is a phonetic approximation of the sound of the tribal name.

AT THE END

MARCH 18, 1997

5. Biannca Pace's business is The Crystal Gallery, 14-16 Nurses Walk, The Rocks, Sydney, NSW, 2000, Australia.

GLOSSARY

Anasazi

Anasazi is the name for the ancestral Puebloans who lived and farmed in the "Four Corners" area of the United States (Utah, Colorado, Arizona and New Mexico) from approximately A.D. 1 to 1300. Their primary crops were corn, beans and squash. The Anasazi are known for their remarkable building techniques, and many of the structures they built, from pit houses to multi-storied cliff dwellings, remain as a tribute to their architectural abilities. The Anasazi were also highly skilled potters, and beautiful decorated bowls, ladles, mugs and other intricate items have been found in sites throughout the Four Corners area. There are many theories about why the Anasazi gradually abandoned the area by A.D. 1300. Their movement may have been related to drought, climatic change, soil erosion, overuse of the area's resources, or, as Lorraine Mafi-Williams contends, to return to the stars due to the wickedness prevalent on Planet Earth.

Assimilation Policy

The Assimilation Policy was formulated by the Australian government in the 1930s to forcibly integrate Aboriginal people into the mainstream society of Australia. In order to do this, children were taken away from their parents and placed in institutions. The policy made many Aborigines alien to their own culture and traditions, and it has only been since 1967, when the policy was officially abandoned, that the persons belonging to what are called "the stolen generations" have been relinking to their heritage without government interference.

1967 Referendum

The 1967 Referendum removed two discriminatory sections from the Australian Constitution. One section had prevented Aboriginal people from being counted in the official census, meaning they did not officially count as citizens. The other section excluded the Aboriginal people's well-being as a consideration in the Parliament's decision-making of laws for the peace, order and good government of the Commonwealth. More than 90% of the Australian people approved these constitutional changes, the largest referendum majority in Australia's history.

Boamie (aka Rainbow Serpent) see Rainbow Serpent

Co-create

With another or others, to cause to come into being as something unique. Equality, respect for the abilities and contributions of other co-creators, mutuality, and complementary benefit for all involved are intended in the co-creative process.

Dalai Lama

His Holiness the 14th Dalai Lama, Tenzin Gyatso, is the head of state and spiritual leader of the Tibetan people. He was born in 1935 and at the age of two was recognized as the incarnation of the 13th Dalai Lama, Thubten Gyatso. "Dalai Lama" is a Mongolian title meaning "Ocean of Wisdom," and the Dalai Lamas are manifestations of the Bodhisattva of Compassion. Bodhisattvas are enlightened beings who choose to rebirth (reincarnate) to serve humanity. In 1950, His Holiness the Dalai Lama was called upon to assume full political power after China's invasion of Tibet in 1949. Finally, in 1959, the Dalai Lama was forced to escape into exile, and since then has been living in Dharamsala, in north India, the seat of the Tibetan government-in-exile. In 1989, the Dalai Lama was awarded the Nobel Peace Prize for his non-violent struggle for the liberation of Tibet. He also became the first Nobel Laureate to be recognized for his concern for global environmental problems. In May 1990, His Holiness saw the realization of a truly democratic government for the exiled Tibetan community. Based on a 1963 draft for reform, there is now a new Tibetan democratic constitution, based on freedom of speech, belief, assembly and movement.

The constitution is administered by elected members living on the Indian sub-continent and in more than 33 other countries. When Tibet becomes free, the first responsibility of the new interim government will be to undertake the adoption of Tibet's democratic constitution. On that day His Holiness will transfer all his historical and political authority to the interim President and live as an ordinary citizen, a "simple Buddhist monk" whose message is love, compassion, and forgiveness.

Deva

A Sanskrit word that is commonly used for the organizing intelligence of an aspect of nature, or nature spirit.

Didgeridoo

An Aboriginal musical instrument that was originally known to the tribes of the East Kimberly and the northern third of the Northern Territory. Traditionally, a didgeridoo was an instrument played only by men. The didgeridoo is an unstopped hollowed piece of bamboo or termite-hollowed wood, usually the latter, usually from three to five feet long and two or more inches in internal diameter, with a mouthpiece made of wax or hardened gum. The player blows into the instrument in trumpet fashion, using a breathing process called *circular breathing* to create a continuous sound. The didgeridoo is used, with other instruments such as the Bull Roarer and Click Sticks, as an accompaniment to Aboriginal song and dance and in ceremonial functions.

Double-terminated crystal

Crystals that have points on both ends, allowing energy to flow readily in both directions, are called "double-terminated." Double-terminated crystals strengthen energy flow, and in metaphysical or healing practices are especially used when one is sharing or exchanging energy with another person. Double-terminated quartz crystals are considered an important tool to inner self-discovery because of their ability to connect the outer *seeking* personality with the inner *knowing* consciousness. In shamanic applications they are considered gateways to the inner spirit realm, and are frequently used in dreamtime rituals and power dream ceremonies. Those double-terminated quartz crystals that possess unusual clarity, luster, and clean terminations (end points) are especially sought after for their abilities to convey an exchange of energy between the soul consciousness and the human personality.

Dreamtime

The Dreamtime refers to the Aboriginal Creation Myths. According to Mudrooroo in *Aboriginal Mythology*, the Dreamtime symbolizes that all life is part of one interconnected system of relationships that came into existence with the stirrings of the great eternal archetypes, the spirit ancestors who emerged during the Dreamtime. At the beginning, when the Earth was a featureless plain, or, in some myths, covered with water, these archetypes, the creative ancestors, in many shapes and forms, stirred and found themselves in the void—the featureless landscape, the waveless ocean, the cloudless sky. Their stirrings created the landscape that we know today. These creative ancestors are responsible for everything that is, including the names of all things, laws, customs and languages that order the different Aboriginal tribes and communities. The creative period of the Dreamtime is as much metaphysical as an epoch in time. Aboriginal people can bring into the present the spiritual energy of those times by engaging in rituals that the ancestors taught and which connect to the archetypal timelessness of the Dreaming, when all things are made and continue to be made.

Goanna

Goanna is the common name in Australia for a lizard in the family of *Varanidae,* and is often used interchangeably with *monitor lizard* or *varanid.* Varanids range in length from the pygmy species in Australia, with adult total lengths of as little as eight and a quarter inches, to ten feet for the Komodo dragon of Eastern Indonesia. Varanids have evolved into a number of species, and have become specialized for some very different lifestyles. Goanna is one of the mythical Dreamtime Ancestors of the Aboriginal people, and is associated with traditional stories and the formation of sacred sites across Australia.

Grid System *See Rainbow Serpent, Ley lines and Songlines.*

Harmonic Convergence

The event called the Harmonic Convergence apparently had

its origins in the book *The Mayan Factor* by Jose Arguelles, published in early 1987. Arguelles' text argued that during a critical time (August 16-17, 1987, when an astrological conjunction of a number of planets occurred), the prophecies of the Bible and Aztec and Mayan calendars indicated that the world would enter a twenty-five year period of transition to world evolution. The purpose of the Harmonic Convergence was to create a global signal of a synchronized human intention to act on behalf of a positive future for Planet Earth. One of the central themes of the Harmonic Convergence was the expansion of consciousness.

Heyokah Medicine

The Divine Trickster is called Heyokah by the Plains Tribes (Native Americans). With the help of his Medicine Ally, Coyote, Heyokah is the contrary clown who holds total wisdom and teaches through laughter and opposites, often creating lessons at the expense of another's seriousness. Laughter is the ultimate lesson that diminishes fear, uproots stasis in people, and tricks them into enlightened states of understanding. Heyokah knows that a willingness to laugh and have others laugh with us will achieve the ultimate union of opposites, when we learn to celebrate more than we mourn and find pleasure in the sacredness of being human.

Humpy

"Humpy" is one of several names for a traditional Aboriginal domed-shaped sleeping shelter made of tree branches woven with leaves. The word "humpy" can also mean any temporary, makeshift dwelling built of whatever found materials are at hand.

Lemuria/Lemurian

Lemuria was an ancient civilization that existed prior to and during the time of Atlantis. Physically, it is believed Lemuria existed largely in the Southern Pacific, between North America and Asia/Australia. Lemuria is also sometimes referred to as Mu, or the Motherland (of Mu). At its peak of civilization, the Lemurian people were said to be both highly evolved and very spiritual. Concrete physical evidence of this ancient continent may be difficult to find, although its existence is documented in ancient texts from many different cultures across the globe. There are certain land masses on the planet that are said to be the last remains of the great Lemurian Empire, such as the Fiji Islands, Hawaii, Easter Island, and some of the Los Angeles area.

Ley Lines

The word "ley" is said to be derived from a Saxon word for "cleared glade," and is also linked to the word "lea," meaning a track of open ground. The term "ley lines" was coined by Alfred Watkins when explaining his theory that ancient sites around Britain had actually been constructed or formed to align between and across the inhabited landscape of Britain.

The sites mentioned include stone circles, standing stones, long barrows, cairns, burial mounds and churches. Others further contend that leys mark paths of some sort of Earth energy that is detectable and was perhaps sensed by early humans. This energy is compared to the flow of *chi*, the universal life force identified in ancient Chinese philosophy.

Rainbow Serpent (aka *Boamie*)

According to Lorraine Mafi-Williams, in the old ways of the Aboriginal people, the Rainbow Serpent is a protective grid covering the Earth called "Boamie." The rainbow colors of Boamie reflect the beauty of the earth and sky, as well as veins of magnetically sensitive minerals and crystals with energy fields that flow similar to blood flowing in the veins of living creatures. Mining interests deplete these precious metals and jeopardize the stability of the energy grid. The Rainbow Serpent of the Aboriginal Dreamtime is associated with both male and female characteristics. The Serpent Dreaming (archetype) may be considered the fount of all magical power and wisdom.

Sai Baba

Sathya Sai Baba is a prominent spiritual leader and educator in India today. He encourages individuals to dedicate their lives to service to humanity and to practice the universal virtues of truth, right conduct, peace, universal love and non-violence. He has inspired the formation in India of a major university system, which is tuition-free, and also the development of an "education in human values" program that teaches universal values accepted by all religious and philosophical systems. This curriculum is taught in schools worldwide. Another major aspect of his work in India involves the establishment of a service organization and charitable activities, particularly in the area of health care. Great interest in the life and teachings of Sathya Sai Baba has resulted in the formation of over 6,500 Centers in over 137 countries, where his teachings are studied and service to the community is emphasized.

Sirius

Sirius (from the Greek *Seirios,* "scorching"), also called the Dog Star, the brightest star in the sky, is situated in the constellation Canis Major. The brilliance of Sirius is in large part a consequence of its relative nearness to the Earth. Irregularities in the motion of Sirius led the German astronomer Friedrich Bessel to believe that the star (Sirius A) was accompanied by an unseen companion star (Sirius B), which was detected in 1862 by the American astronomer Alvan Clark. The existence of this companion star, although unrecognized in western astronomy, had been known for centuries by the Dogon tribe of Mali, whose tradition records early contact with visitors from Sirius. Sirius was highly venerated by the ancient Egyptians, and many Egyptian temples were constructed in such a way that the light of Sirius reached the inner chambers. Sirius is also an aspect of the Aboriginal Dreamtime stories, several of which link the origins of the stars Sirius and the star Canopus. The hottest part of the summer coincides with the heliacal rising of Sirius, and thus acquired the name "dog days."

Songlines

Aborigines possess an acute sensitivity to magnetic and vital force flows emanating from the earth, which they refer to as "songlines." Songlines are maps recorded in song depicting mythic events of the Dreamtime at successive sites along a walking trail that winds through a region. They detail the travels of the Dreamtime Ancestors, and each verse describes the geographical features of the landscape. Encoded within the songlines are the great ceremonies that reactivate the Dreamtime in the present. Groups of individuals with the same Dreamings are bonded by a common link to the spiritual, and share songlines across Australia. Also, each Aboriginal tribe inherits a network of songlines. All travel in the lands of neighboring tribes is done along these lines. As songlines stretch in all directions across the entire continent of Australia, they form a network of communication and cultural exchange among peoples separated by great distances.

The Summer of Love

The Summer of Love evolved out of the first great Human Be-In in San Francisco's Golden Gate Park in early 1967. The organizers' intent for the Be-In was to unite mainstream activists with the laidback hippie culture. Drawing 35,000 people, it featured Timothy Leary, Allen Ginsberg, poet Gary Snyder, Dick Gregory, and all the local rock bands. Realizing that a possible result of the Be-In would be to attract a huge number of young people to the Haight-Asbury area when schools let out in April or May, several of the original organizers set up the Council for the Summer of Love specifically to mitigate, in a very practical and generous way, some of the problems that would predictably accompany such a population explosion. They worked closely with local churches, health clinics, runaway and homeless shelters, and musical and artistic events to help young people network with each other in order to find food and shelter and keep out of trouble. The term "Summer of Love" was an attempt to balance the media's negative images of the 1960s nascent cultural renaissance with a more positive alignment of intention — that is, to celebrate humane, compassionate and democratic ideals.

Uluru

Located near Alice Springs in the Red Center of Australia, Uluru is the Aboriginal name for Ayers Rock, perhaps the only place of pilgrimage in Australia visited by people of all races and all nationalities. Uluru is sacred to Aboriginal people all across Australia, for here the many songlines and Dreaming tracks come together in a unity of mythic celebration. Uluru is a giant sandstone monolith rising more than 1,300 ft above the surrounding desert. There is a sunny side and a shady side, signifying the division between two great myth cycles, when opposites met in a great battle that marks the end of the Dreamtime saga and the beginning of our own age. The scars and marks on the sides of Uluru record these events.

Wollumbin

Wollumbin is the Aboriginal name for Mount Warning, named so by Captain Cook as a landmark for avoiding Point Danger off Tweed Heads. The mountain is located in the northern part of New South Wales and is the former central magma chamber of an ancient massive volcano that once covered an area of approximately 1,545 square miles. The top of Wollumbin is the first part of Australia touched by the rising sun each day. Wollumbin is a sacred Aboriginal site for men, although women in Lorraine's clan are its traditional custodians and only women are able to activate the giant rose quartz crystal at its center, thereby representing the balance of male and female energy. In Aboriginal Lore, Wollumbin has long been known by Aborigines to actually belong to Native Americans, although it remained connected to Australia when the first great planetary land mass split apart.

Universal Horn

"Universal Horn" is an instrument newly invented by the Tibetan musician Nawang Khechog. The Universal Horn is a combination of Tibetan long horn, Australian Aboriginal didgeridoo, and American trombone.

BIBLIOGRAPHY

Anthony, Carol K. *A Guide to the I Ching:* Third Edition, Revised and Enlarged. Stow, MA: Anthony Publishing Company, 1988.

Chatwin, Bruce. *The Songlines.* New York: Penguin Books, 1987.

Lawlor, Robert. *Voices of the First Day: Awakening in the Aboriginal Dreamtime.* Rochester, VT: Inner Traditions, 1991.

Lee, Scout Cloud, Ed.D. *The Circle Is Sacred: A Medicine Book For Women.* Tulsa, OK: Council Oak Books, 1995.

Lonely Planet Travel Survival Kit: Australia, 1977. Victoria, Australia: Lonely Planet Publications, 1996.

McFadden, Steven. *Ancient Voices, Current Affairs: The Legend of the Rainbow Warriors.* Santa Fe, NM: Bear & Company, 1992.

Murphet, Howard. *Walking the Path with Sai Baba.* 1983. York Beach, ME: Samuel Weiser, 1993.

——. *Sai Inner Views and Insights: 30 Years with the Avatar.* Fabar, VA: Leela Press, 1996.

——. *Sai Baba, Man of Miracles.* New York Beach, ME: Samuel Weiser, 1977.

Nyoongah, Mudrooroo. *Aboriginal Mythology.* London: Thorsons-HarperCollins, 1994.

Raphael, Katrina. *The Crystalline Transmission: A Synthesis of Light: Volume III.* Santa Fe, NM: Aurora Press, 1990.

Shute, Nevil. *On the Beach,* 1957. New York: Ballentine Books, 1997.

——. *A Town Like Alice,* 1950. New York: Ballentine Books, 1991.

Spirit Song. Compiled by Lorraine Mafi-Williams. Norwood, South Australia: Omnibus Books-Ashton Scholastic Group, 1993.

ENJOY · ENLARGE · ENLIGHTEN · ENLIVEN
your Self

For more information about Anne Richardson Williams or *Unconventional Means: The Dream Down Under*, or to find other inspirational and empowering books published by Pearlsong Press:

go to:	www.pearlsong.com
call:	1-866-4-A-PEARL
or write to	Pearlsong Press
	P.O. Box 58065
	Nashville, TN 37205

www.ingramcontent.com/pod-product-compliance
Lightning Source LLC
Chambersburg PA
CBHW032049080426
42733CB00006B/218

9 781597 190015